The 3-Minute PRINCESS Leadership Journal for Girls

✏ THIS AWESOME JOURNAL BELONGS TO:

Blank Classic

The 3-Minute Princess
        Leadership Journal for Girls
116 numbered pages - 120 total pages
A5 (5.83 x 8.27)

Blank Classic

Mailing address:
Blank Classic
PO BOX 4608
Main Station Terminal
349 West Georgia Street
Vancouver, BC
Canada, V6B 4A1

Cover design by: Lauren Dick
Interior design by: Lauren Dick

ISBN: 978-1-77476-185-4

FIRST EDITION / FIRST PRINTING

I CAN ...
SHOW KINDNESS
SET GOALS
BE A GOOD LISTENER
INSPIRE PEOPLE
LEARN FROM OTHERS
BELIEVE IN MYSELF
SET A GOOD EXAMPLE
EMBRACE DIFFERENCES
ADMIT MISTAKES
HELP PEOPLE
BECAUSE I AM A LEADER
SIGNED,

DATE: S M T W TH F S __ / __ / __

OVERALL TODAY WAS: ☆ ☆ ☆ ☆ ☆

👍 TODAY'S TRIUMPHS

👎 TODAY'S CHALLENGES

💡 WHAT I LEARNED FROM TODAY:

🏆 MY TOP GOAL FOR TOMORROW:

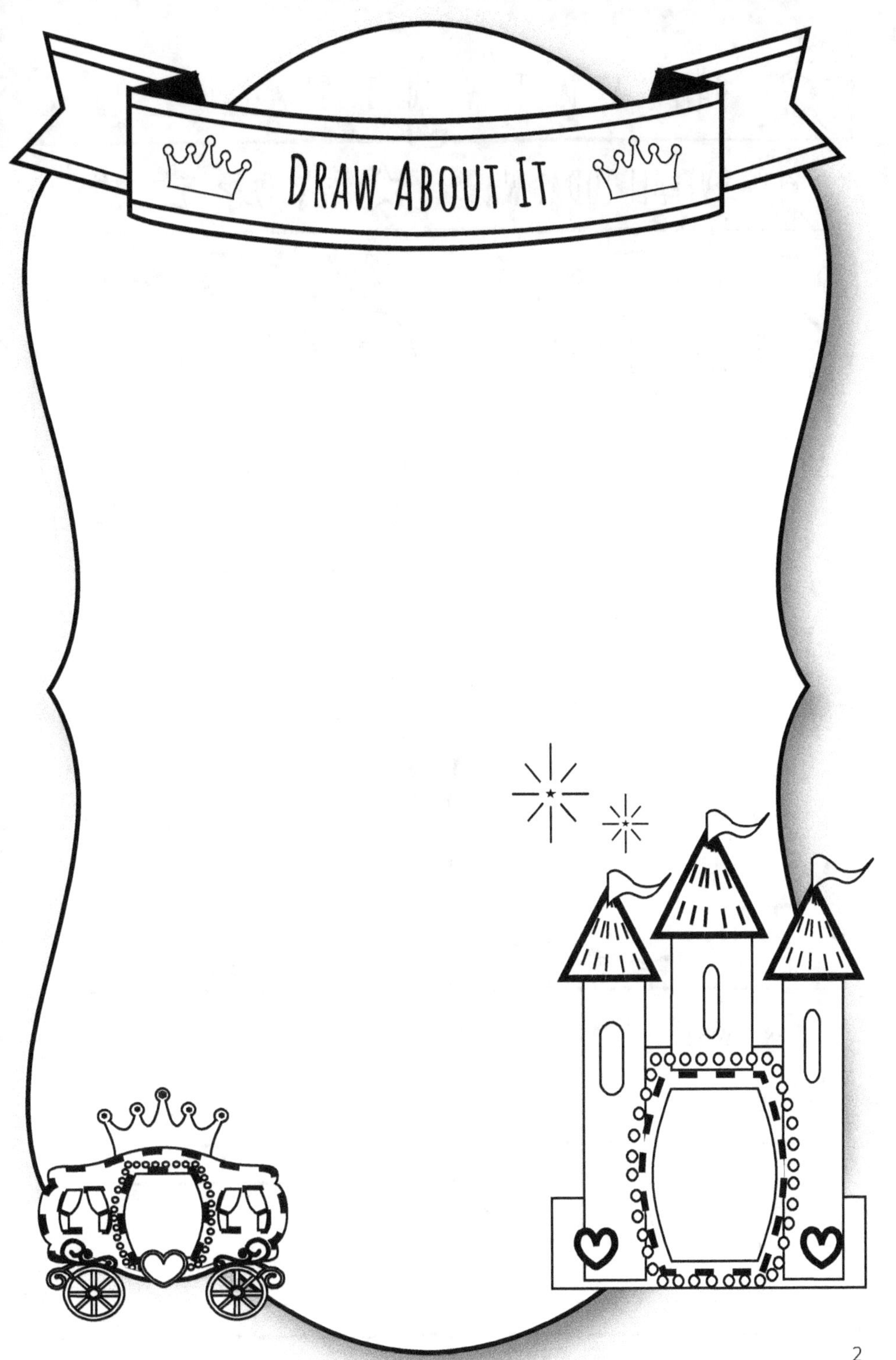
Draw About It

DATE: S M T W TH F S __ / __ / __

OVERALL TODAY WAS: ☆ ☆ ☆ ☆ ☆

👍 TODAY'S TRIUMPHS

👎 TODAY'S CHALLENGES

💡 WHAT I LEARNED FROM TODAY:

🏆 MY TOP GOAL FOR TOMORROW:

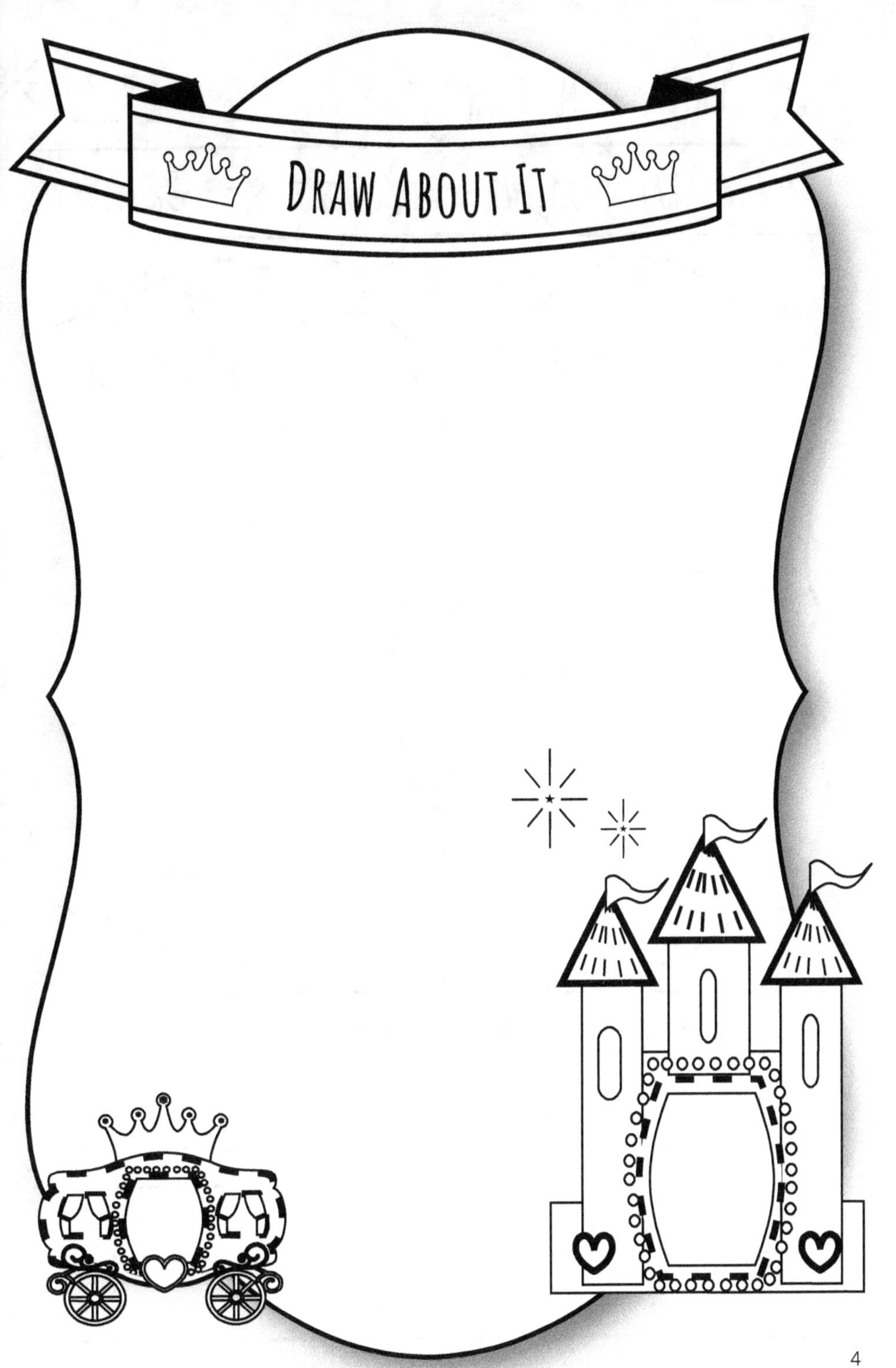
Draw About It

DATE: S M T W TH F S   __ / __ / __

OVERALL TODAY WAS: ☆ ☆ ☆ ☆ ☆

👍 TODAY'S TRIUMPHS

👎 TODAY'S CHALLENGES

💡 WHAT I LEARNED FROM TODAY:

🏆 MY TOP GOAL FOR TOMORROW:

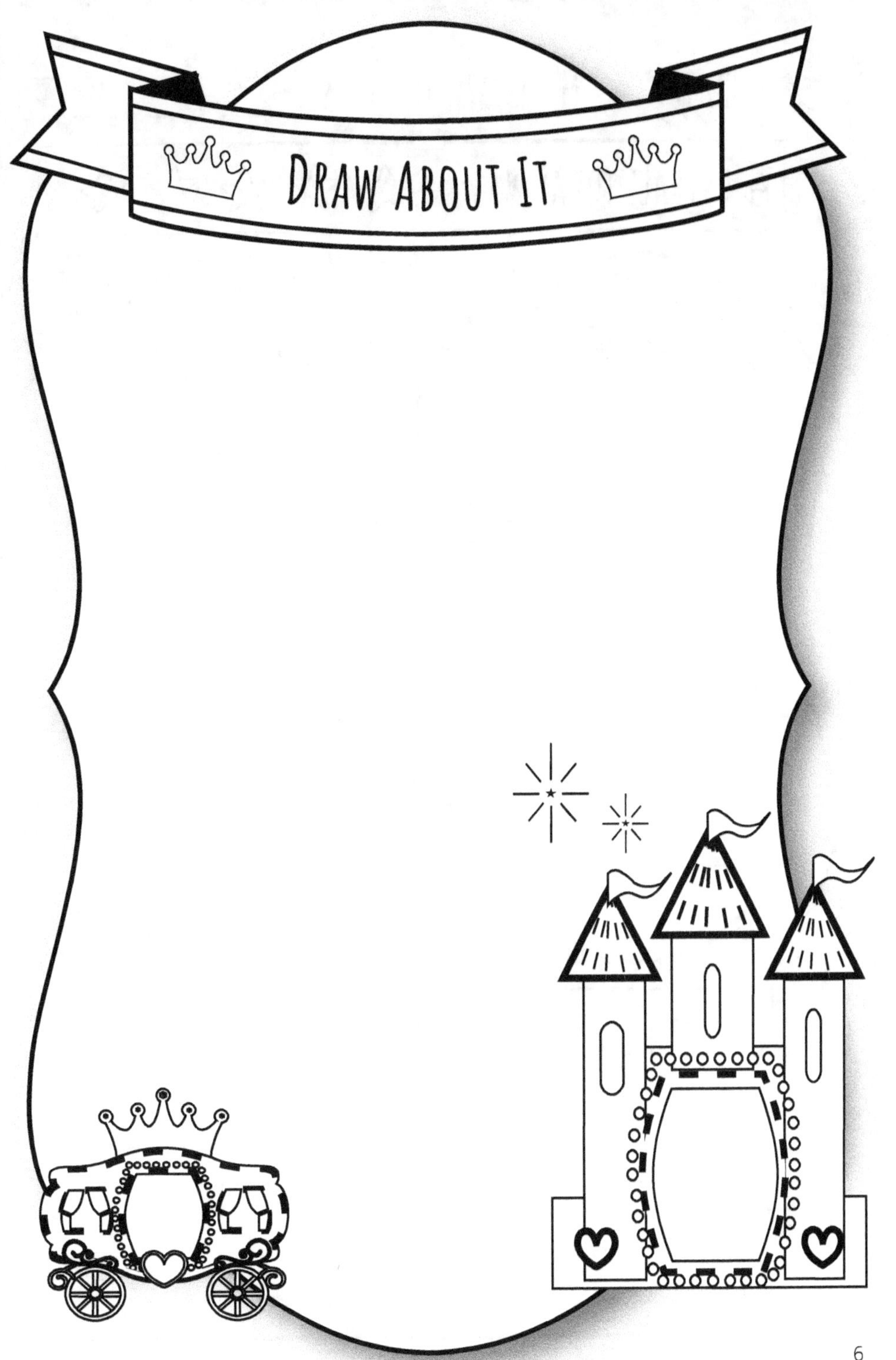

DRAW ABOUT IT

DATE: S M T W TH F S __ / __ / __

OVERALL TODAY WAS: ☆ ☆ ☆ ☆ ☆

👍 TODAY'S TRIUMPHS

👎 TODAY'S CHALLENGES

💡 WHAT I LEARNED FROM TODAY:

🏆 MY TOP GOAL FOR TOMORROW:

DRAW ABOUT IT

DATE: S M T W TH F S __ / __ / __

OVERALL TODAY WAS: ☆ ☆ ☆ ☆ ☆

👍 TODAY'S TRIUMPHS

👎 TODAY'S CHALLENGES

💡 WHAT I LEARNED FROM TODAY:

🏆 MY TOP GOAL FOR TOMORROW:

DRAW ABOUT IT

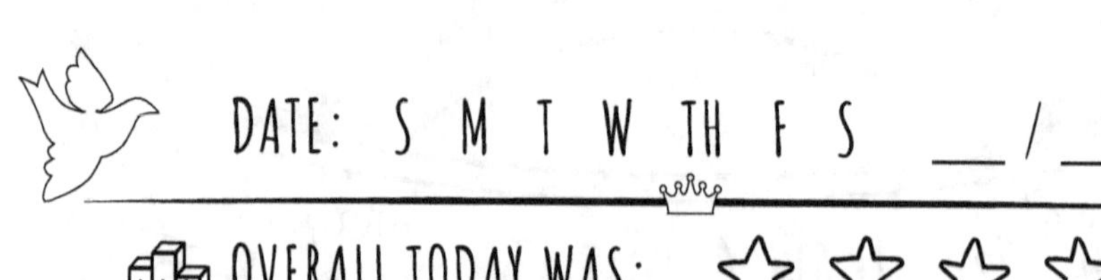

DATE: S   M   T   W   TH   F   S   __ / __ / __

OVERALL TODAY WAS: ☆ ☆ ☆ ☆ ☆

👍 TODAY'S TRIUMPHS

👎 TODAY'S CHALLENGES

💡 WHAT I LEARNED FROM TODAY:

🏆 MY TOP GOAL FOR TOMORROW:

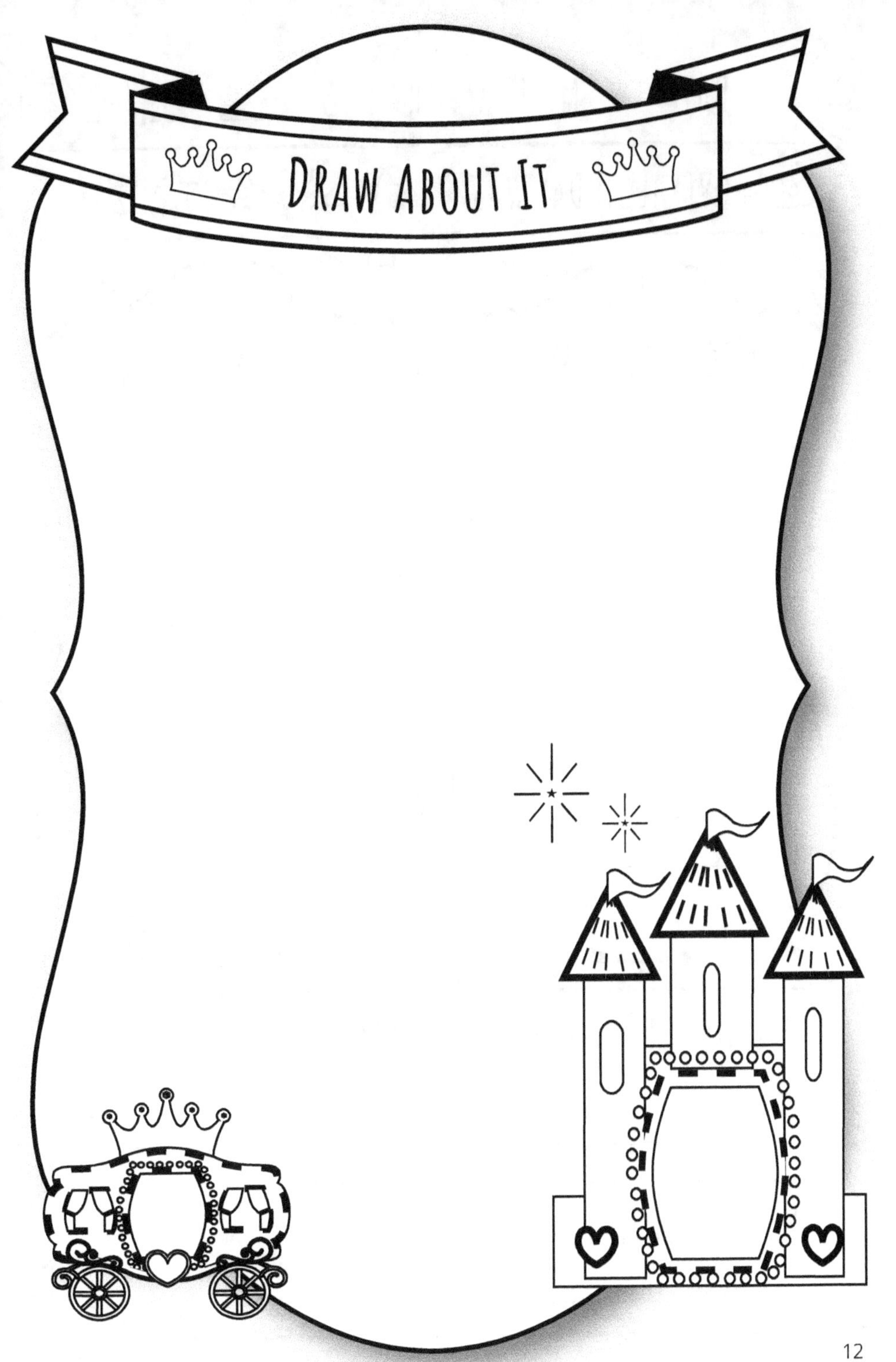
Draw About It

DATE: S M T W TH F S __/__/__

🎖 OVERALL TODAY WAS: ☆ ☆ ☆ ☆ ☆

👍 TODAY'S TRIUMPHS

👎 TODAY'S CHALLENGES

💡 WHAT I LEARNED FROM TODAY:

🏆 MY TOP GOAL FOR TOMORROW:

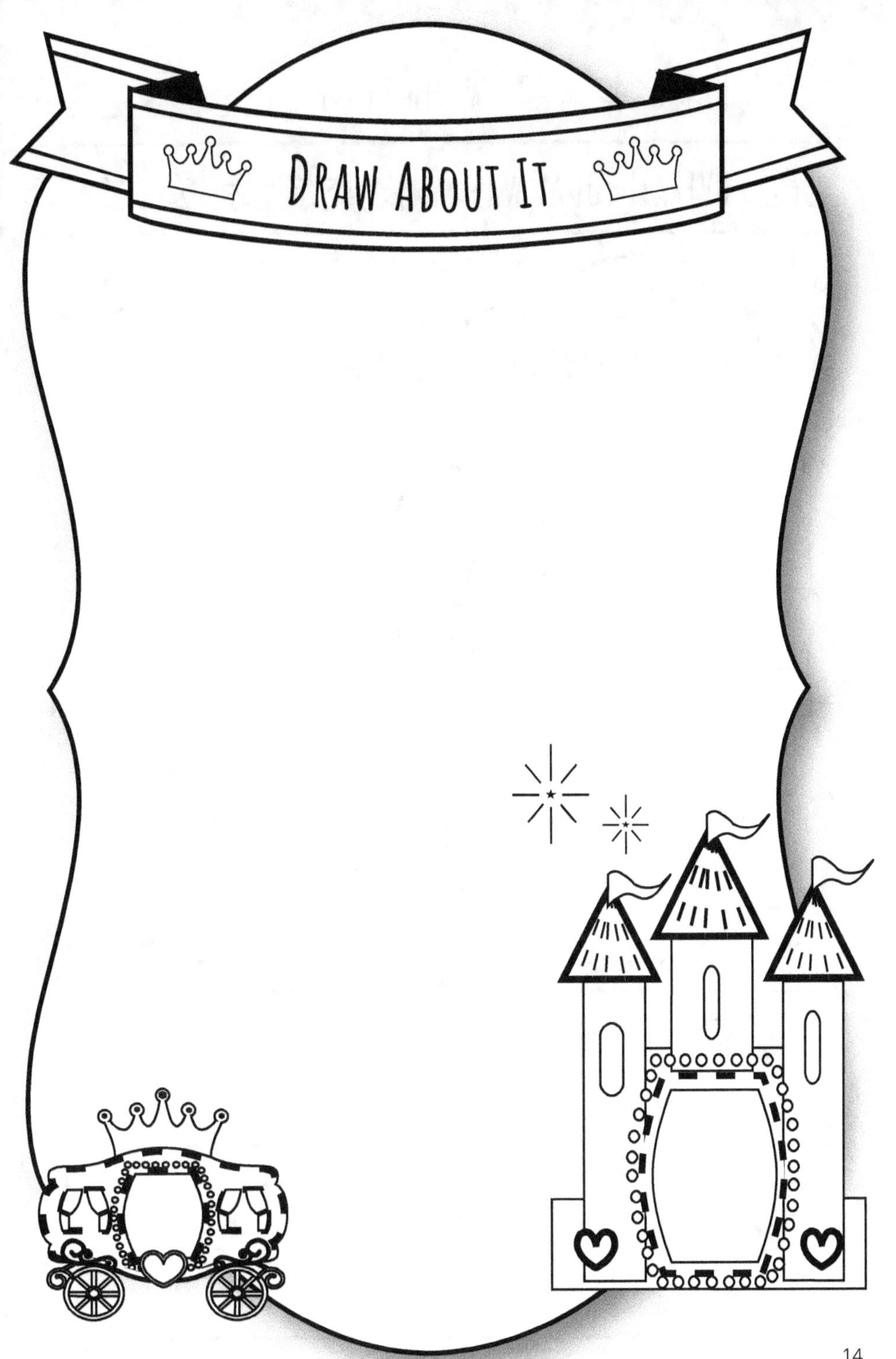
Draw About It

DATE: S M T W TH F S __ / __ / __

OVERALL TODAY WAS: ☆ ☆ ☆ ☆ ☆

👍 TODAY'S TRIUMPHS

____
____
____
____
____
____
____
____
____
____

👎 TODAY'S CHALLENGES

____
____
____
____
____
____
____
____
____

💡 WHAT I LEARNED FROM TODAY:

____
____

🏆 MY TOP GOAL FOR TOMORROW:

____
____

Draw About It

DATE: S M T W TH F S __ / __ / __

OVERALL TODAY WAS: ☆ ☆ ☆ ☆ ☆

TODAY'S TRIUMPHS

TODAY'S CHALLENGES

WHAT I LEARNED FROM TODAY:

MY TOP GOAL FOR TOMORROW:

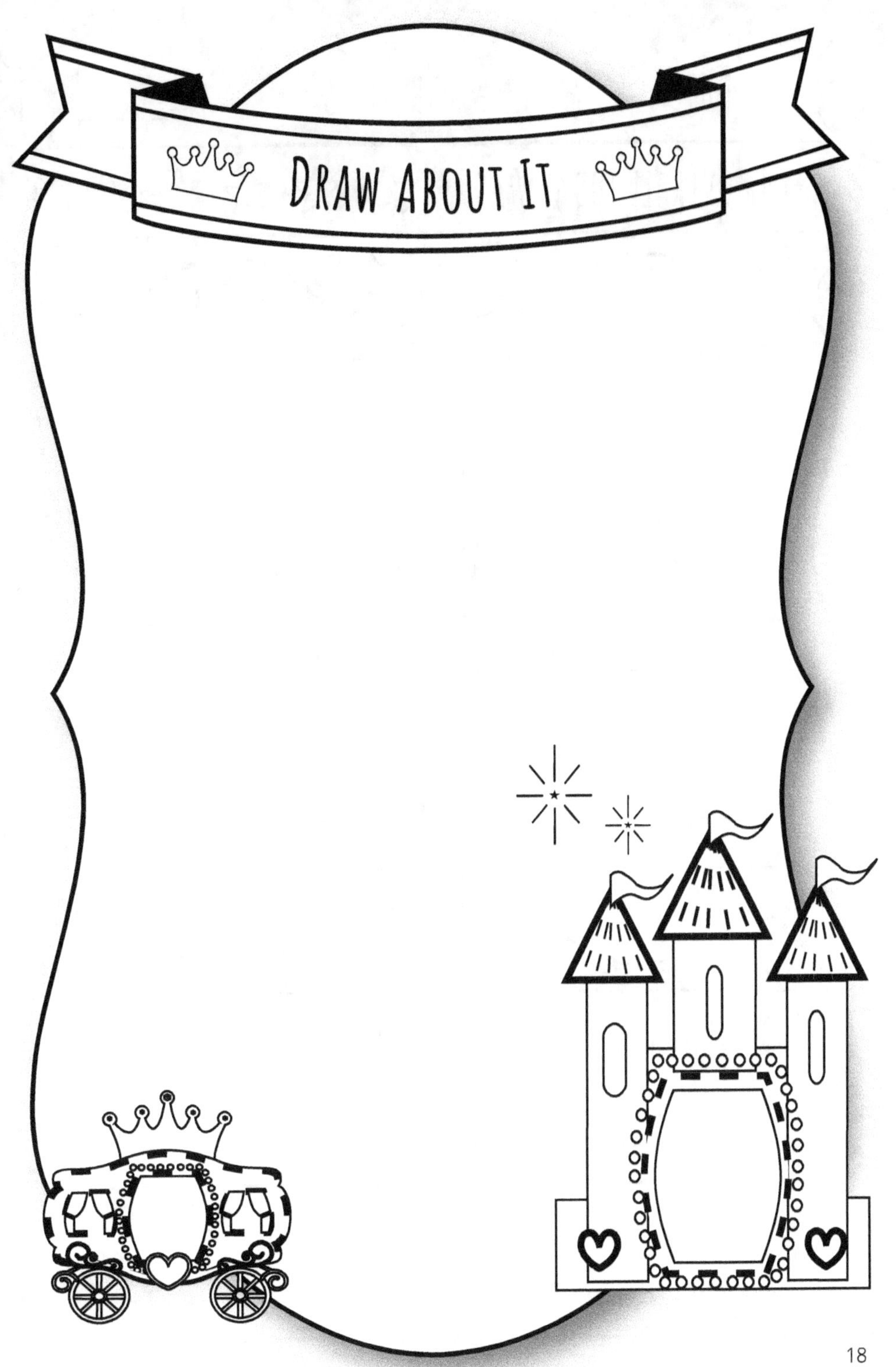
DRAW ABOUT IT

DATE: S M T W TH F S __ / __ / __

🧱 OVERALL TODAY WAS: ☆ ☆ ☆ ☆ ☆

👍 TODAY'S TRIUMPHS

____
____
____
____
____
____
____
____

👎 TODAY'S CHALLENGES

____
____
____
____
____
____
____
____

💡 WHAT I LEARNED FROM TODAY:

____
____

🏆 MY TOP GOAL FOR TOMORROW:

____

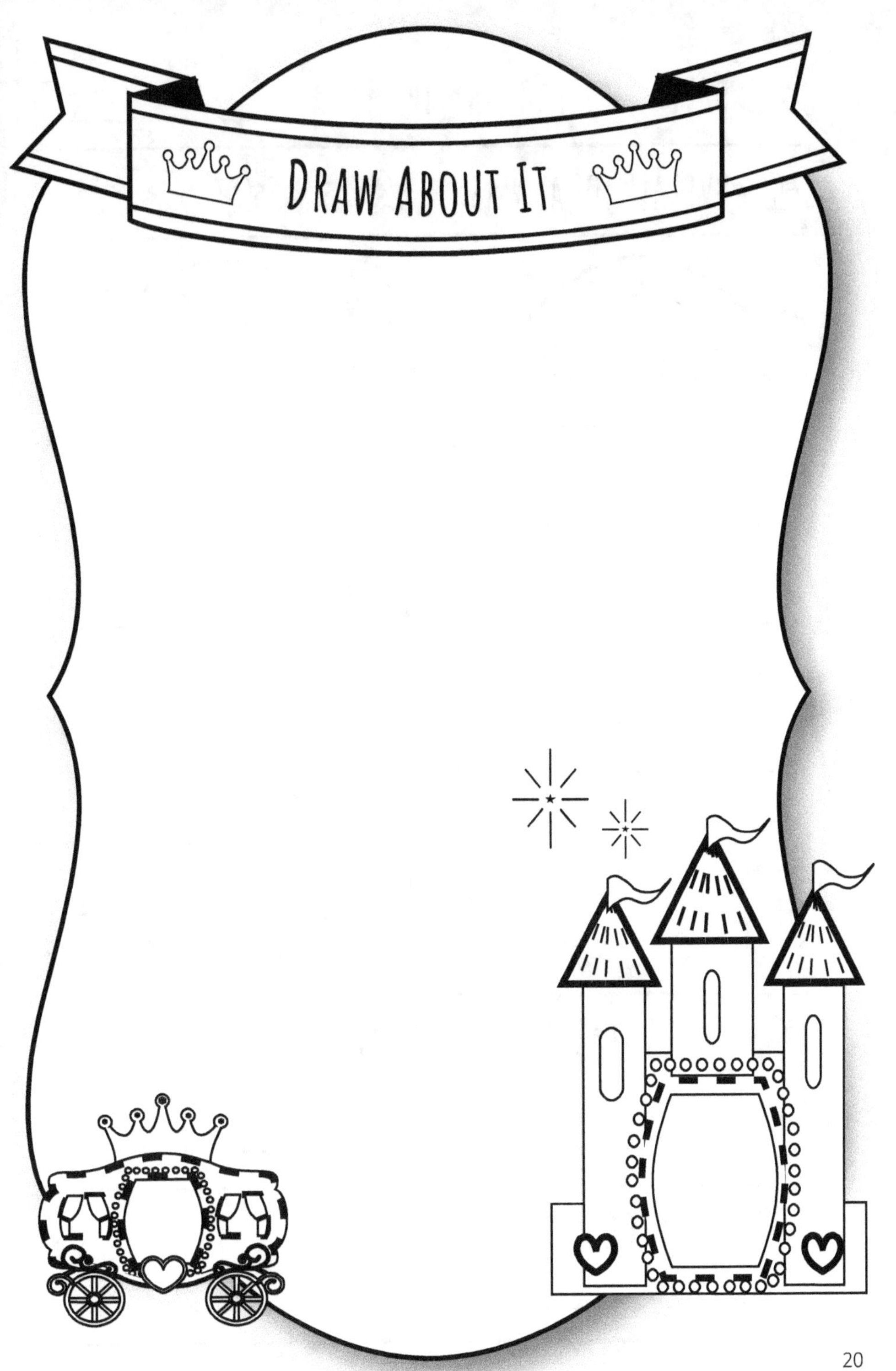
DRAW ABOUT IT

DATE: S M T W TH F S __ / __ / __

OVERALL TODAY WAS: ☆ ☆ ☆ ☆ ☆

👍 TODAY'S TRIUMPHS

____
____
____
____
____
____
____
____
____
____

👎 TODAY'S CHALLENGES

____
____
____
____
____
____
____
____
____
____

💡 WHAT I LEARNED FROM TODAY:

____
____

🏆 MY TOP GOAL FOR TOMORROW:

____
____

DRAW ABOUT IT

DATE: S M T W TH F S __ / __ / __

OVERALL TODAY WAS: ☆ ☆ ☆ ☆ ☆

👍 TODAY'S TRIUMPHS

👎 TODAY'S CHALLENGES

💡 WHAT I LEARNED FROM TODAY:

🏆 MY TOP GOAL FOR TOMORROW:

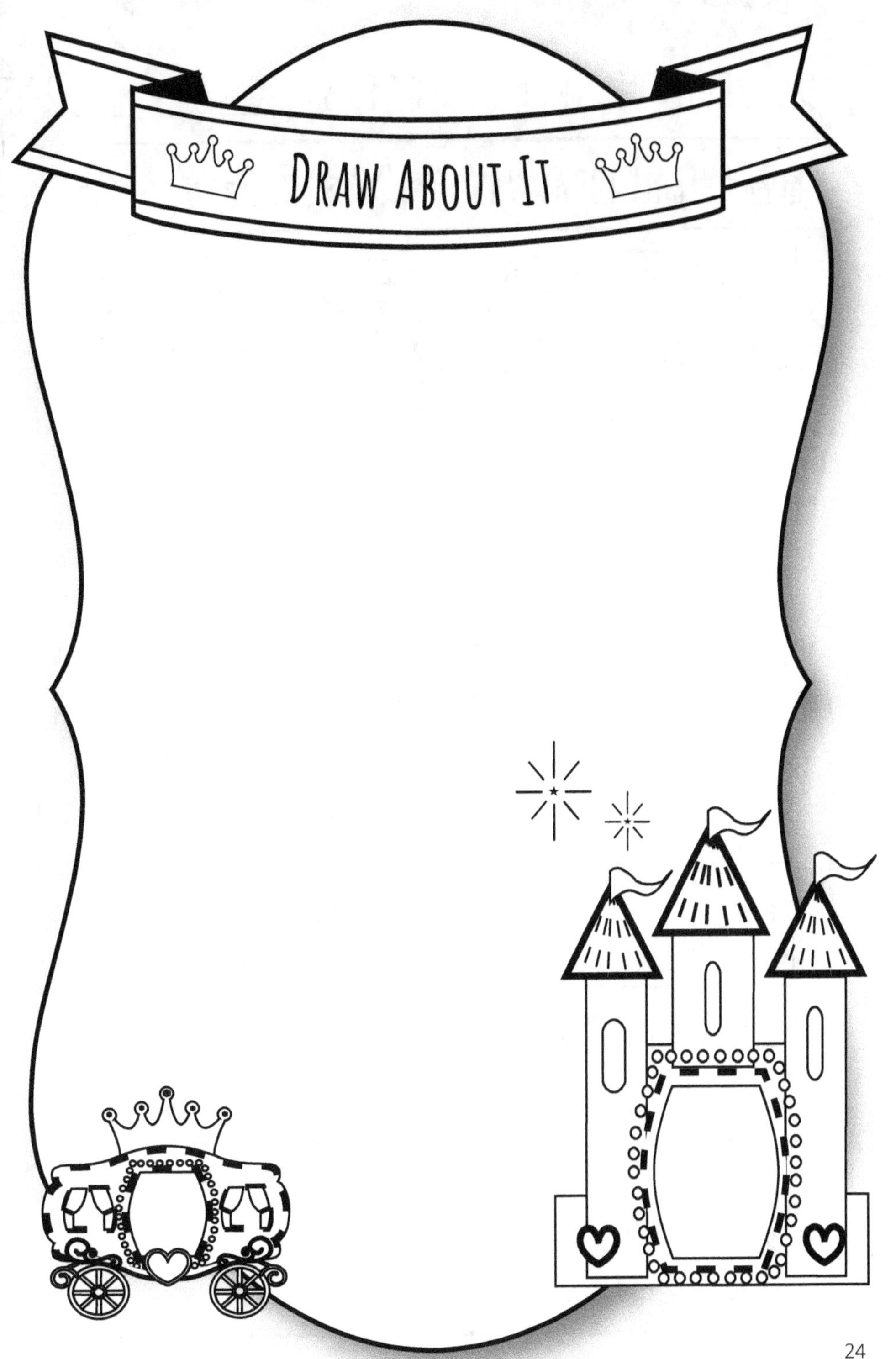
DRAW ABOUT IT

DATE: S M T W TH F S   __ / __ / __

🏆 OVERALL TODAY WAS: ☆ ☆ ☆ ☆ ☆

👍 TODAY'S TRIUMPHS

____
____
____
____
____
____
____
____
____
____

👎 TODAY'S CHALLENGES

____
____
____
____
____
____
____
____
____

💡 WHAT I LEARNED FROM TODAY:

____
____

🏆 MY TOP GOAL FOR TOMORROW:

____
____

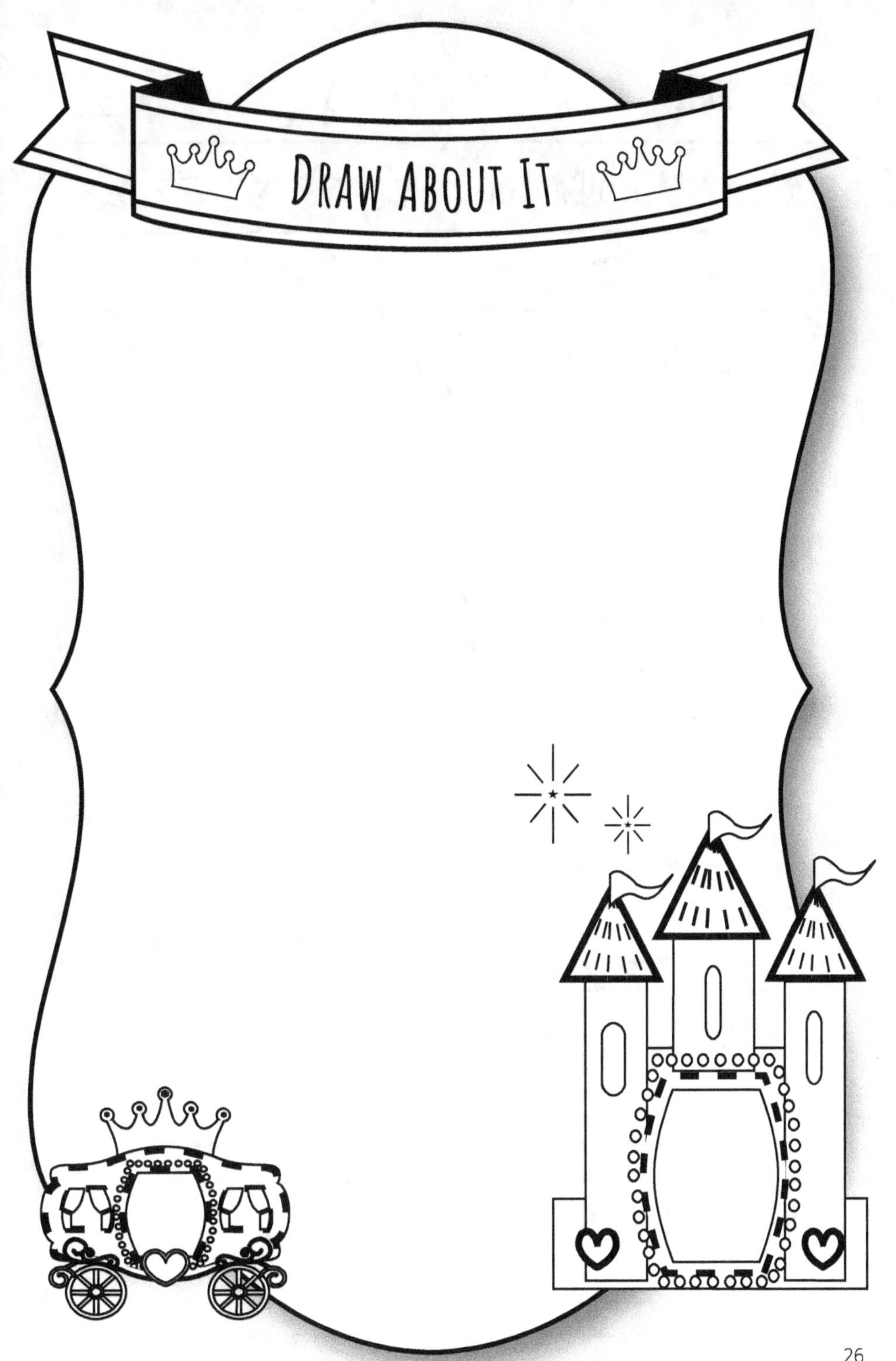
Draw About It

DATE: S M T W TH F S __ / __ / __

OVERALL TODAY WAS: ☆ ☆ ☆ ☆ ☆

👍 TODAY'S TRIUMPHS

👎 TODAY'S CHALLENGES

💡 WHAT I LEARNED FROM TODAY:

🏆 MY TOP GOAL FOR TOMORROW:

DRAW ABOUT IT

DATE: S M T W TH F S __ / __ / __

OVERALL TODAY WAS: ☆ ☆ ☆ ☆ ☆

👍 TODAY'S TRIUMPHS

👎 TODAY'S CHALLENGES

💡 WHAT I LEARNED FROM TODAY:

🏆 MY TOP GOAL FOR TOMORROW:

29

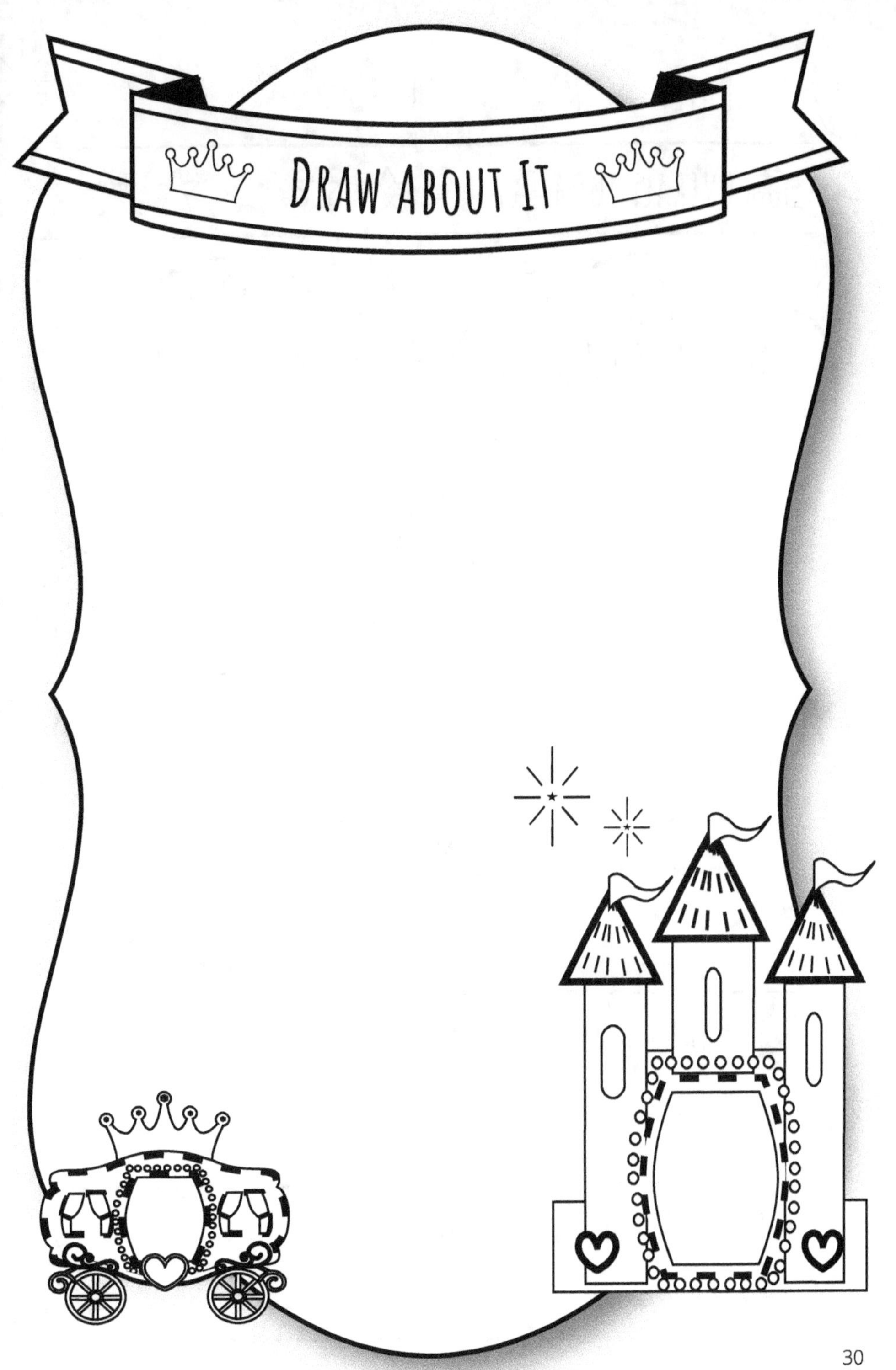

DRAW ABOUT IT

DATE: S M T W TH F S __ / __ / __

🏆 OVERALL TODAY WAS: ☆ ☆ ☆ ☆ ☆

👍 TODAY'S TRIUMPHS

👎 TODAY'S CHALLENGES

💡 WHAT I LEARNED FROM TODAY:

🏆 MY TOP GOAL FOR TOMORROW:

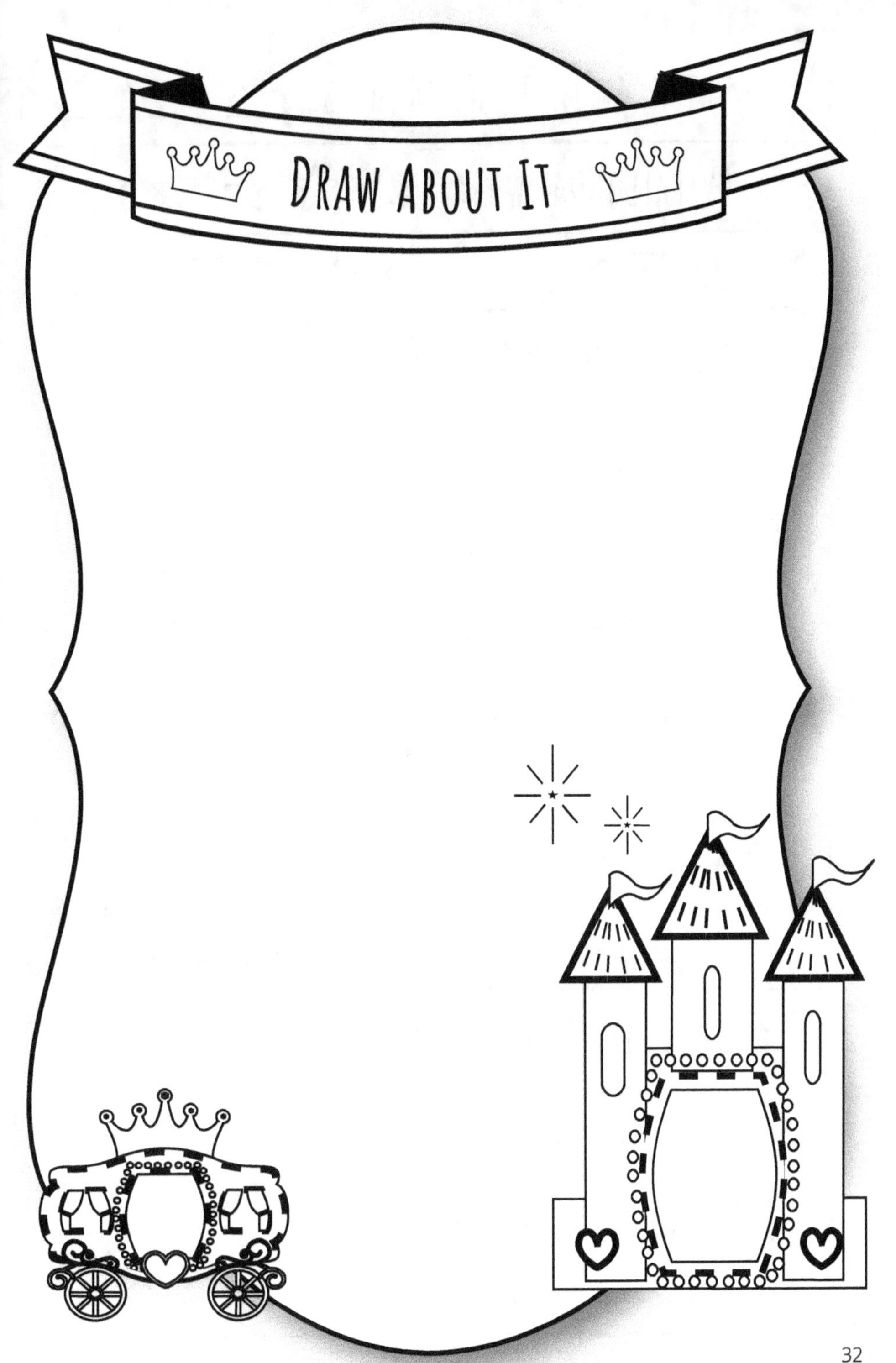
DRAW ABOUT IT

DATE: S M T W TH F S __ / __ / __

TODAY'S TRIUMPHS

TODAY'S CHALLENGES

WHAT I LEARNED FROM TODAY:

MY TOP GOAL FOR TOMORROW:

Draw About It

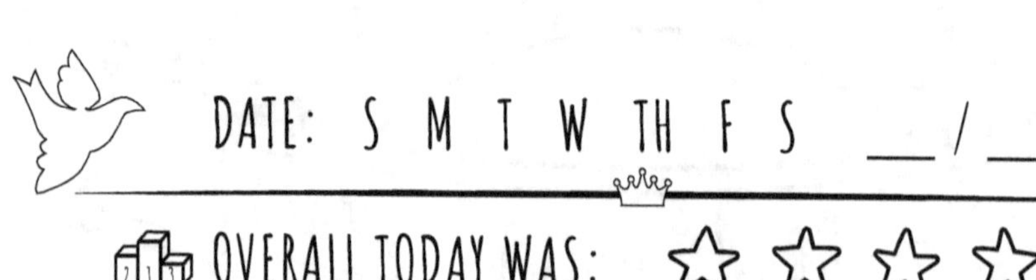

DATE: S M T W TH F S   __ / __ / __

🧱 OVERALL TODAY WAS: ☆ ☆ ☆ ☆ ☆

👍 TODAY'S TRIUMPHS

👎 TODAY'S CHALLENGES

💡 WHAT I LEARNED FROM TODAY:

🏆 MY TOP GOAL FOR TOMORROW:

DRAW ABOUT IT

DATE: S M T W TH F S __/__/__

OVERALL TODAY WAS: ☆ ☆ ☆ ☆ ☆

👍 TODAY'S TRIUMPHS

____
____
____
____
____
____
____
____
____

👎 TODAY'S CHALLENGES

____
____
____
____
____
____
____
____

💡 WHAT I LEARNED FROM TODAY:

____
____

🏆 MY TOP GOAL FOR TOMORROW:

____
____

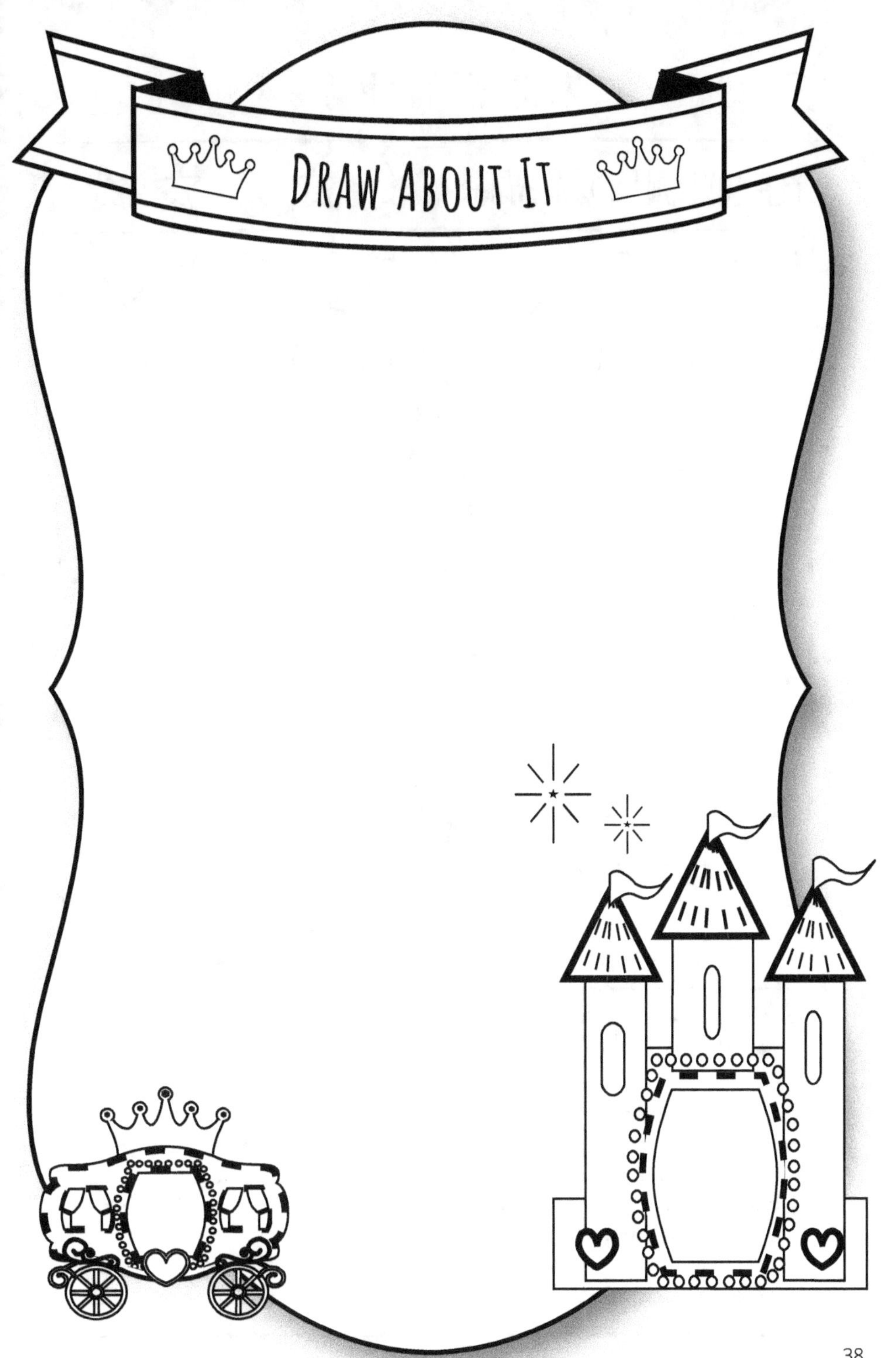
Draw About It

DATE: S M T W TH F S __ / __ / __

OVERALL TODAY WAS: ☆ ☆ ☆ ☆ ☆

👍 TODAY'S TRIUMPHS

____
____
____
____
____
____
____
____
____
____

👎 TODAY'S CHALLENGES

____
____
____
____
____
____
____
____
____
____

💡 WHAT I LEARNED FROM TODAY:

____
____

🏆 MY TOP GOAL FOR TOMORROW:

____

DRAW ABOUT IT

DATE: S M T W TH F S __ / __ / __

 OVERALL TODAY WAS: ☆ ☆ ☆ ☆ ☆

👍 TODAY'S TRIUMPHS

👎 TODAY'S CHALLENGES

💡 WHAT I LEARNED FROM TODAY:

🏆 MY TOP GOAL FOR TOMORROW:

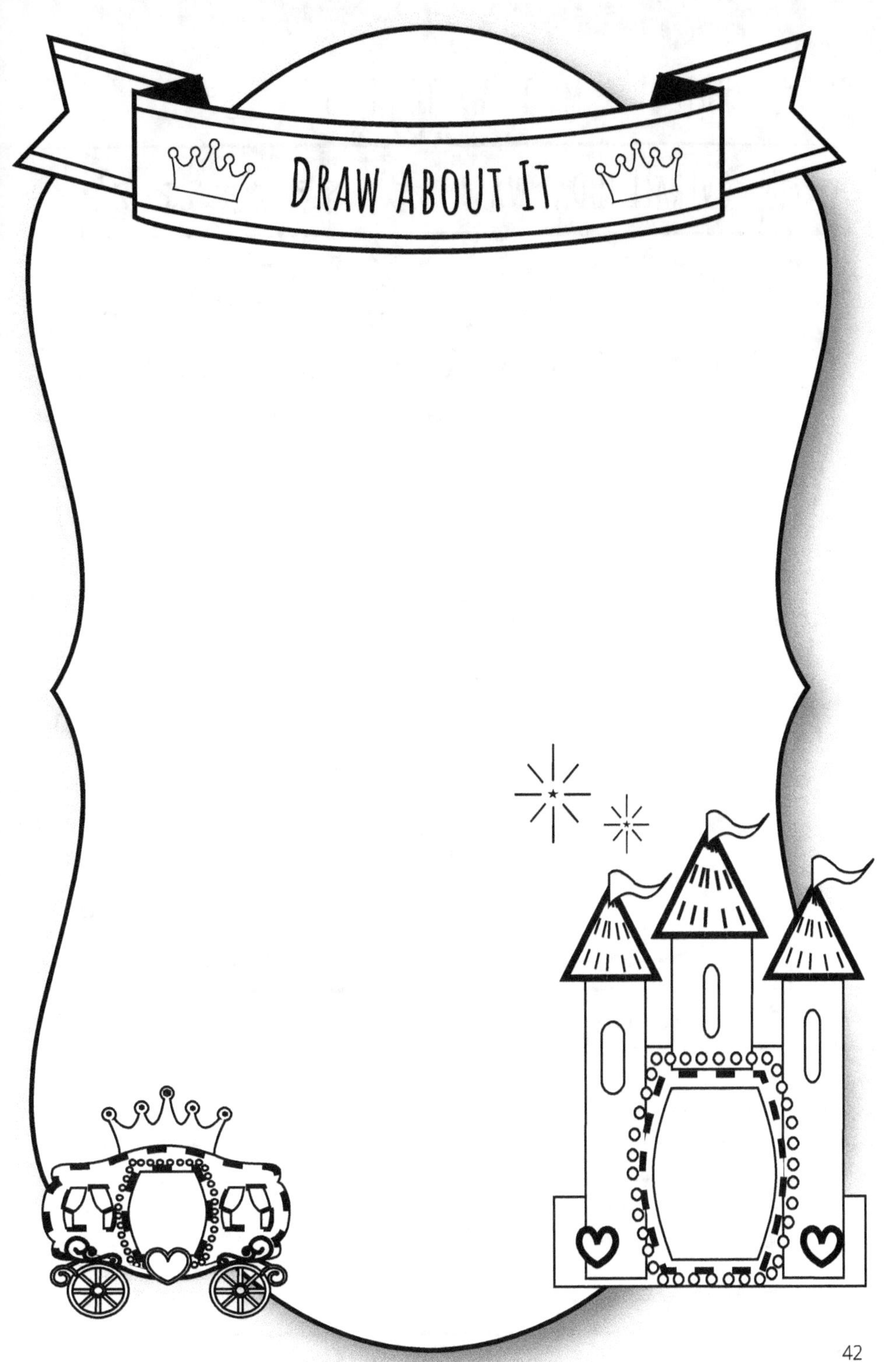

Draw About It

DATE: S M T W TH F S __ / __ / __

OVERALL TODAY WAS: ☆ ☆ ☆ ☆ ☆

TODAY'S TRIUMPHS

TODAY'S CHALLENGES

WHAT I LEARNED FROM TODAY:

MY TOP GOAL FOR TOMORROW:

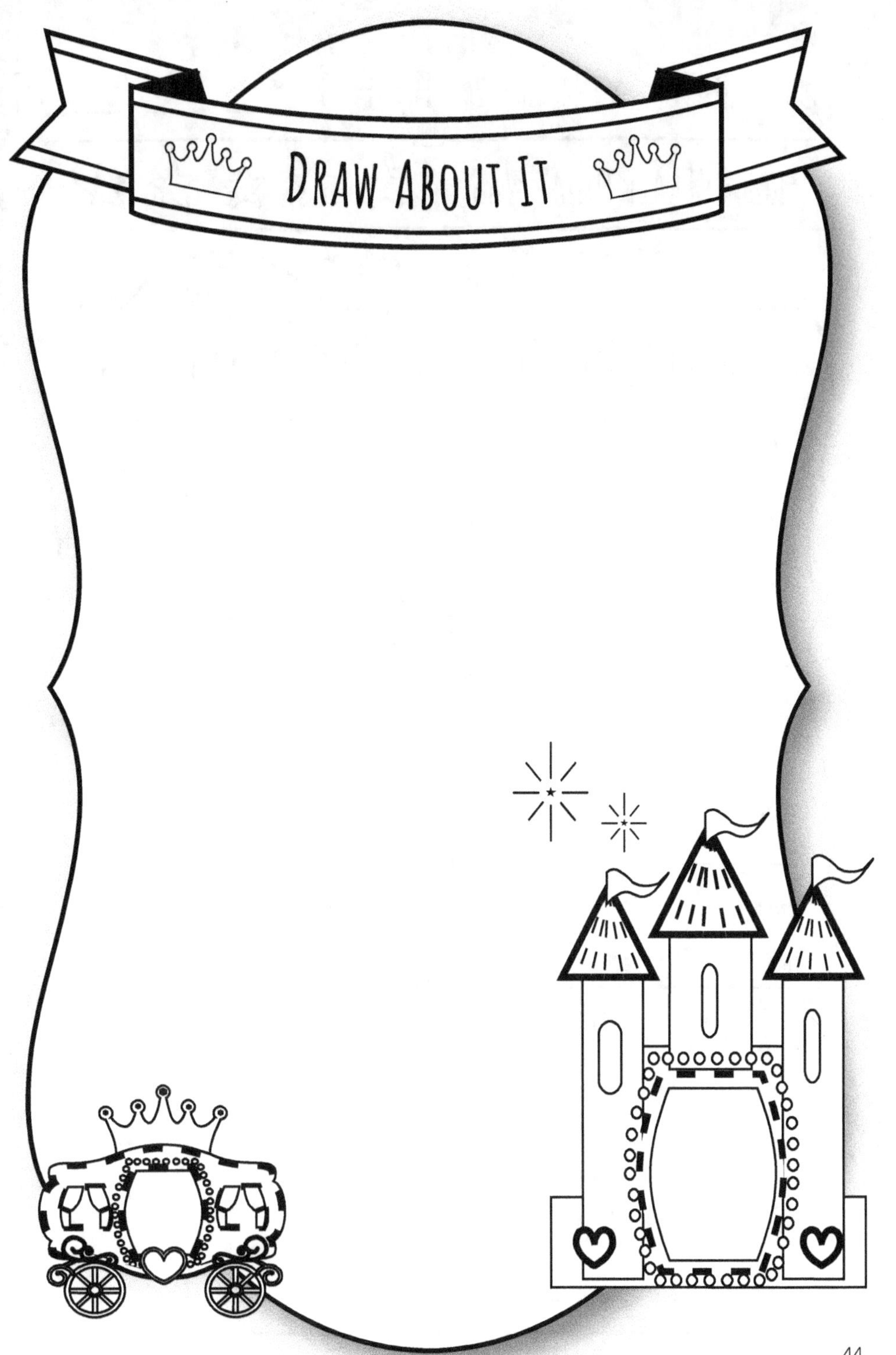

DRAW ABOUT IT

DATE: S M T W TH F S __ / __ / __

OVERALL TODAY WAS: ☆ ☆ ☆ ☆ ☆

👍 TODAY'S TRIUMPHS

👎 TODAY'S CHALLENGES

💡 WHAT I LEARNED FROM TODAY:

🏆 MY TOP GOAL FOR TOMORROW:

Draw About It

DATE: S M T W TH F S __ / __ /__

OVERALL TODAY WAS: ☆ ☆ ☆ ☆ ☆

👍 TODAY'S TRIUMPHS

👎 TODAY'S CHALLENGES

💡 WHAT I LEARNED FROM TODAY:

🏆 MY TOP GOAL FOR TOMORROW:

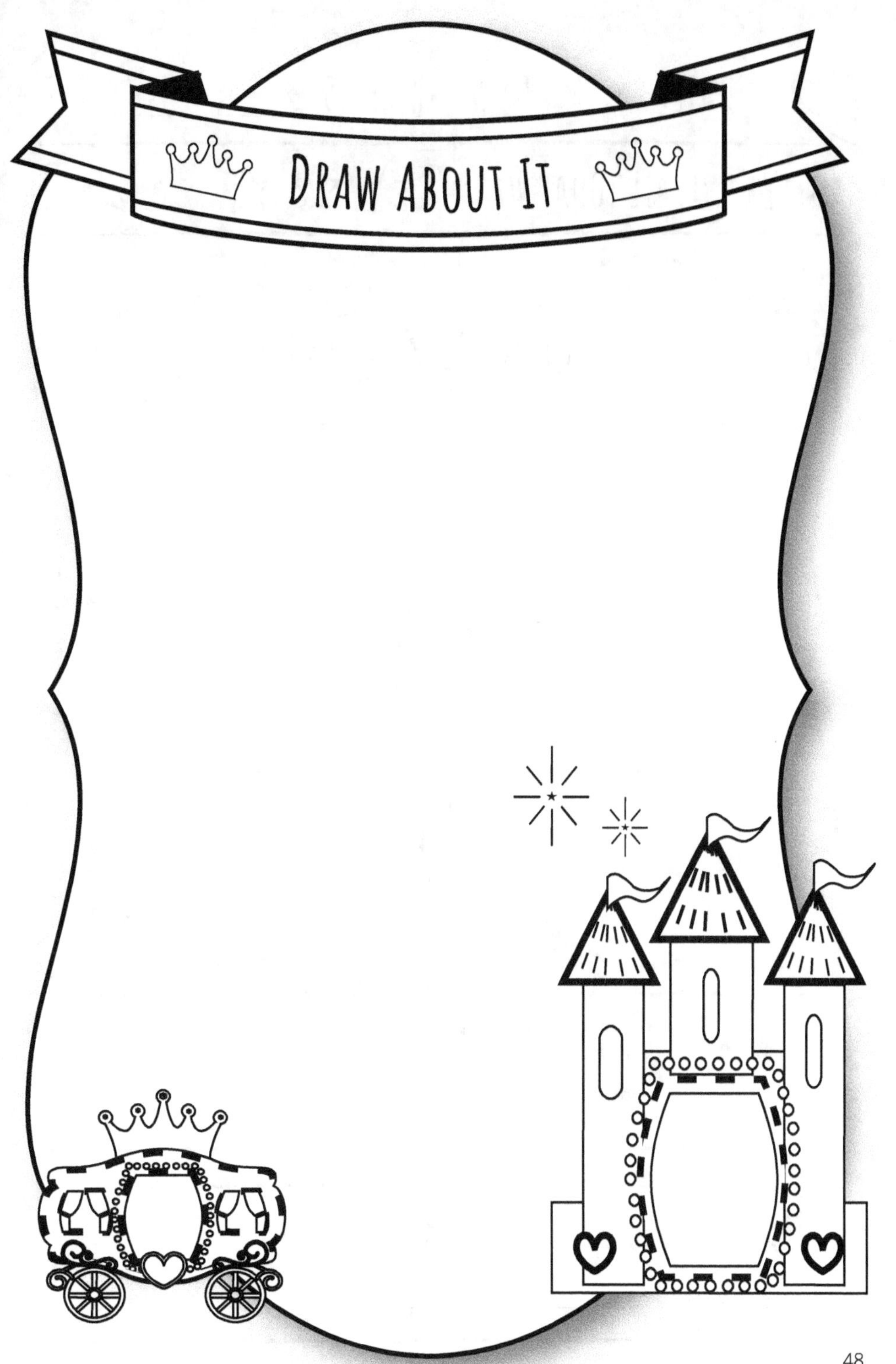
DRAW ABOUT IT

DATE: S M T W TH F S __ / __ / __

OVERALL TODAY WAS: ☆ ☆ ☆ ☆ ☆

TODAY'S TRIUMPHS

TODAY'S CHALLENGES

WHAT I LEARNED FROM TODAY:

MY TOP GOAL FOR TOMORROW:

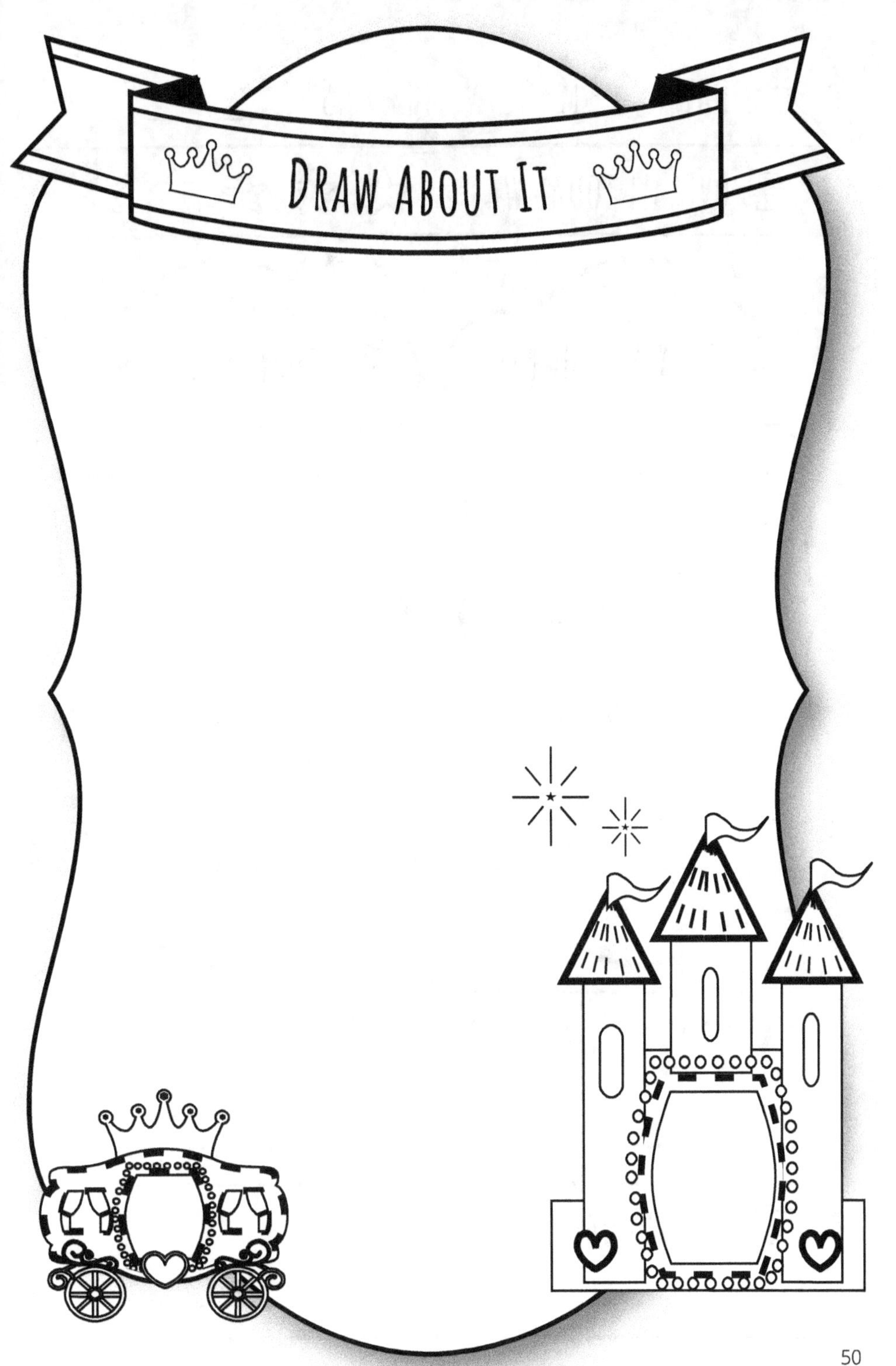
DRAW ABOUT IT

DATE: S M T W TH F S   __ / __ / __

🏆 OVERALL TODAY WAS: ☆ ☆ ☆ ☆ ☆

👍 TODAY'S TRIUMPHS

👎 TODAY'S CHALLENGES

💡 WHAT I LEARNED FROM TODAY:

🏆 MY TOP GOAL FOR TOMORROW:

Draw About It

DATE: S M T W TH F S __/__/__

🎲 OVERALL TODAY WAS: ☆ ☆ ☆ ☆ ☆

👍 TODAY'S TRIUMPHS

____
____
____
____
____
____
____
____

👎 TODAY'S CHALLENGES

____
____
____
____
____
____
____
____

💡 WHAT I LEARNED FROM TODAY:

____
____

🏆 MY TOP GOAL FOR TOMORROW:

____
____

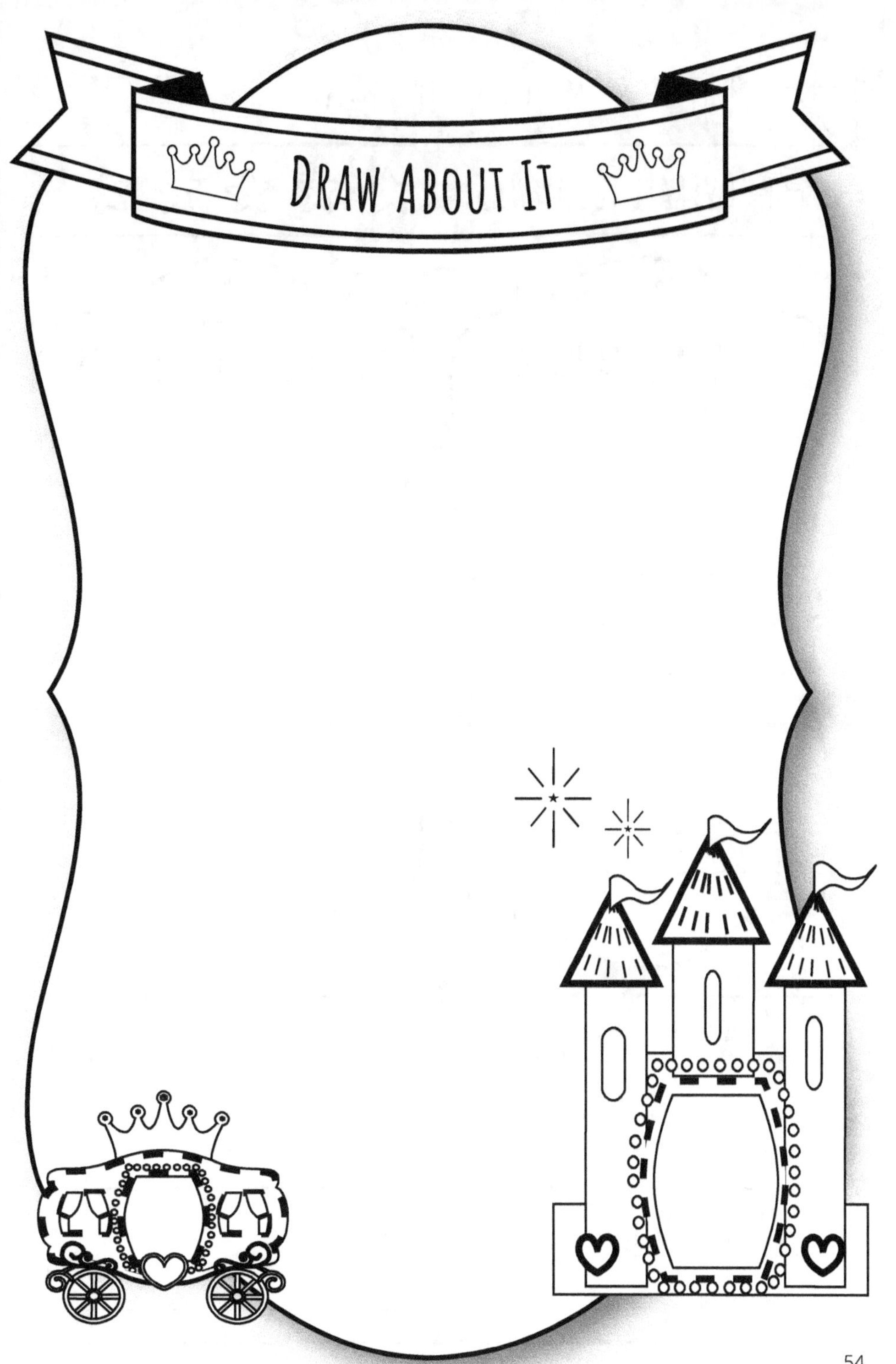

DRAW ABOUT IT

DATE: S M T W TH F S __ / __ / __

🏆 OVERALL TODAY WAS: ☆ ☆ ☆ ☆ ☆

👍 TODAY'S TRIUMPHS

👎 TODAY'S CHALLENGES

💡 WHAT I LEARNED FROM TODAY:

🏆 MY TOP GOAL FOR TOMORROW:

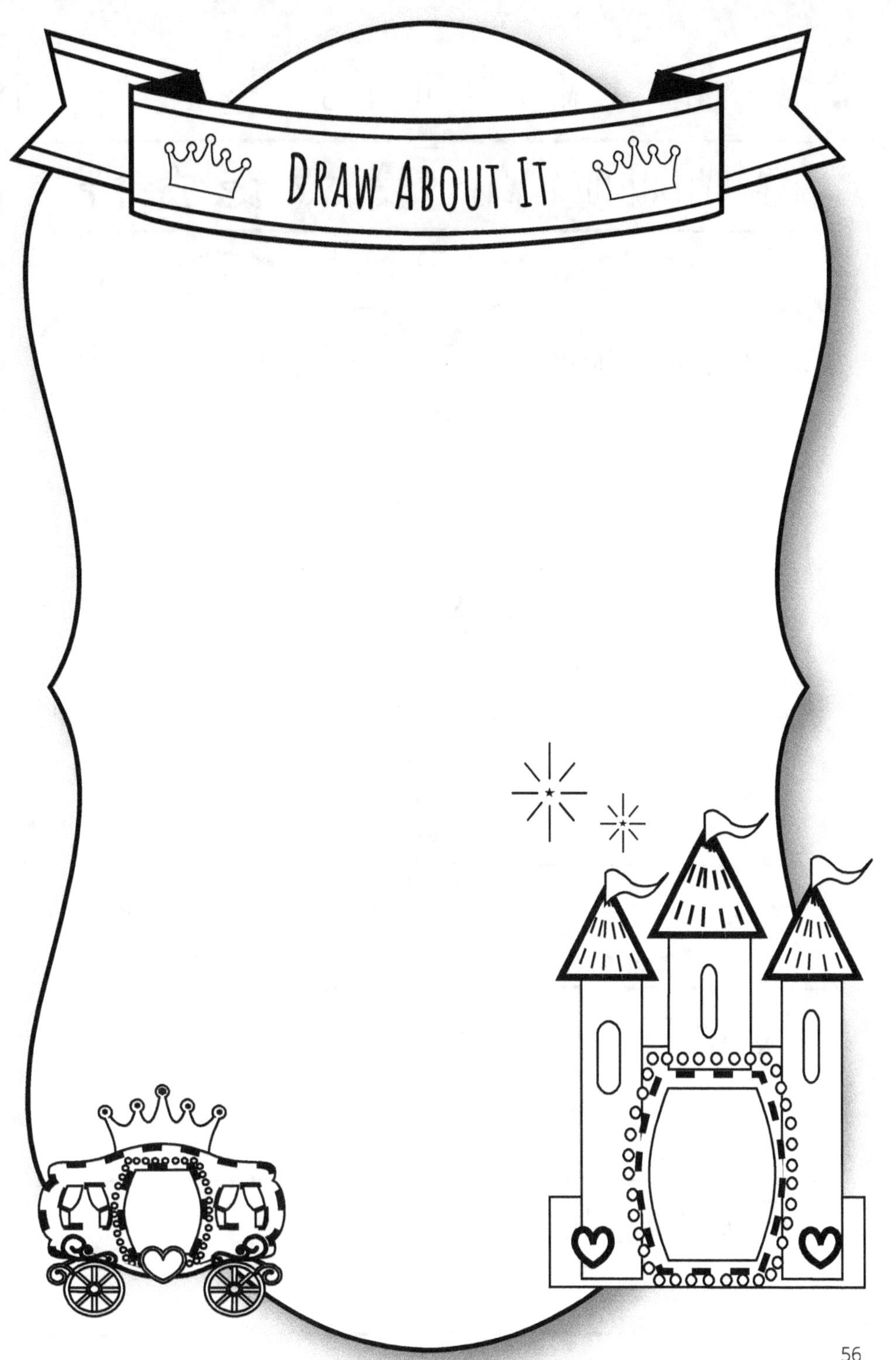
DRAW ABOUT IT

DATE: S M T W TH F S __ / __ / __

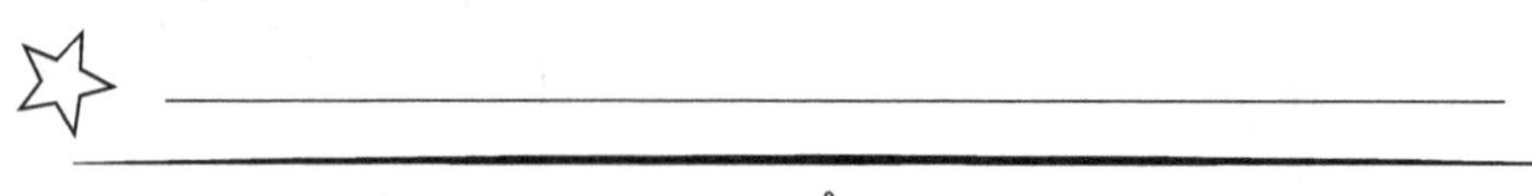

🧱 OVERALL TODAY WAS: ☆ ☆ ☆ ☆ ☆

👍 TODAY'S TRIUMPHS

👎 TODAY'S CHALLENGES

💡 WHAT I LEARNED FROM TODAY:

____

🏆 MY TOP GOAL FOR TOMORROW:

____

DRAW ABOUT IT

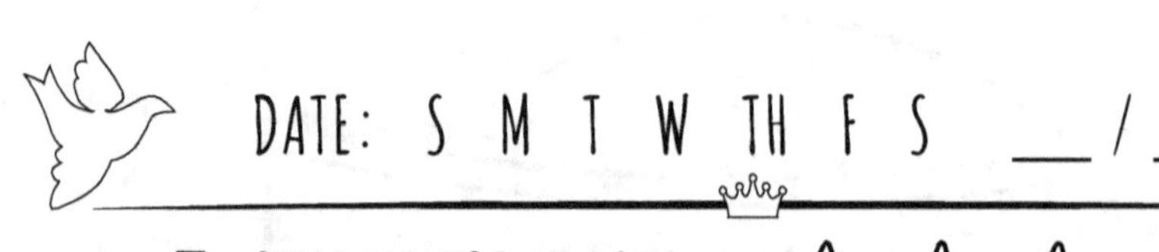

DATE: S M T W TH F S ___ / ___ /___

OVERALL TODAY WAS: ☆ ☆ ☆ ☆ ☆

👍 TODAY'S TRIUMPHS

👎 TODAY'S CHALLENGES

💡 WHAT I LEARNED FROM TODAY:

🏆 MY TOP GOAL FOR TOMORROW:

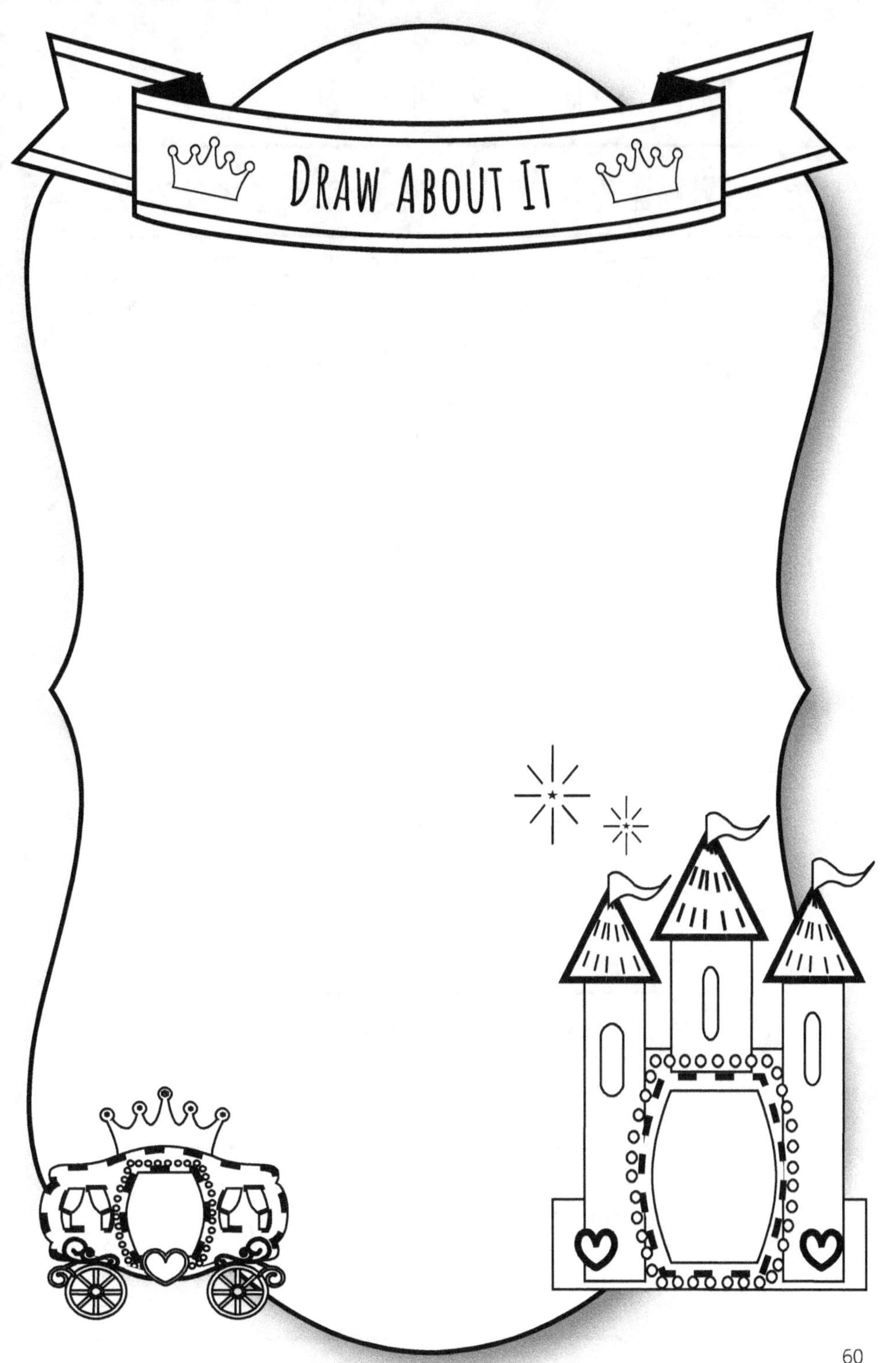

DRAW ABOUT IT

DATE: S M T W TH F S __ / __ / __

OVERALL TODAY WAS: ☆ ☆ ☆ ☆ ☆

👍 TODAY'S TRIUMPHS

👎 TODAY'S CHALLENGES

💡 WHAT I LEARNED FROM TODAY:

🏆 MY TOP GOAL FOR TOMORROW:

Draw About It

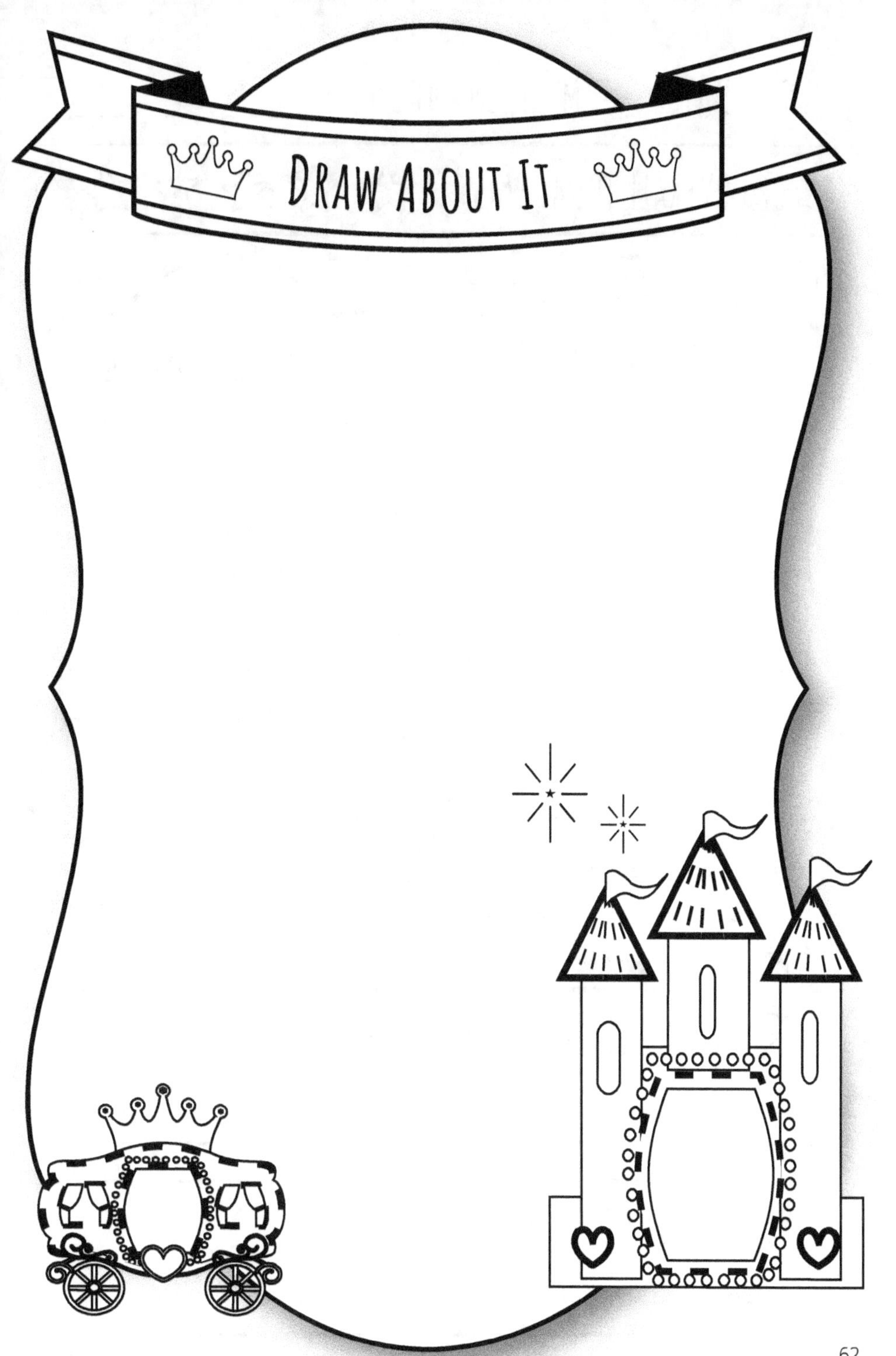

DATE: S M T W TH F S __ / __ / __

OVERALL TODAY WAS: ☆ ☆ ☆ ☆ ☆

TODAY'S TRIUMPHS

TODAY'S CHALLENGES

WHAT I LEARNED FROM TODAY:

MY TOP GOAL FOR TOMORROW:

DRAW ABOUT IT

DATE: S M T W TH F S __ / __ / __

🧱 OVERALL TODAY WAS: ☆ ☆ ☆ ☆ ☆

👍 TODAY'S TRIUMPHS

👎 TODAY'S CHALLENGES

💡 WHAT I LEARNED FROM TODAY:

🏆 MY TOP GOAL FOR TOMORROW:

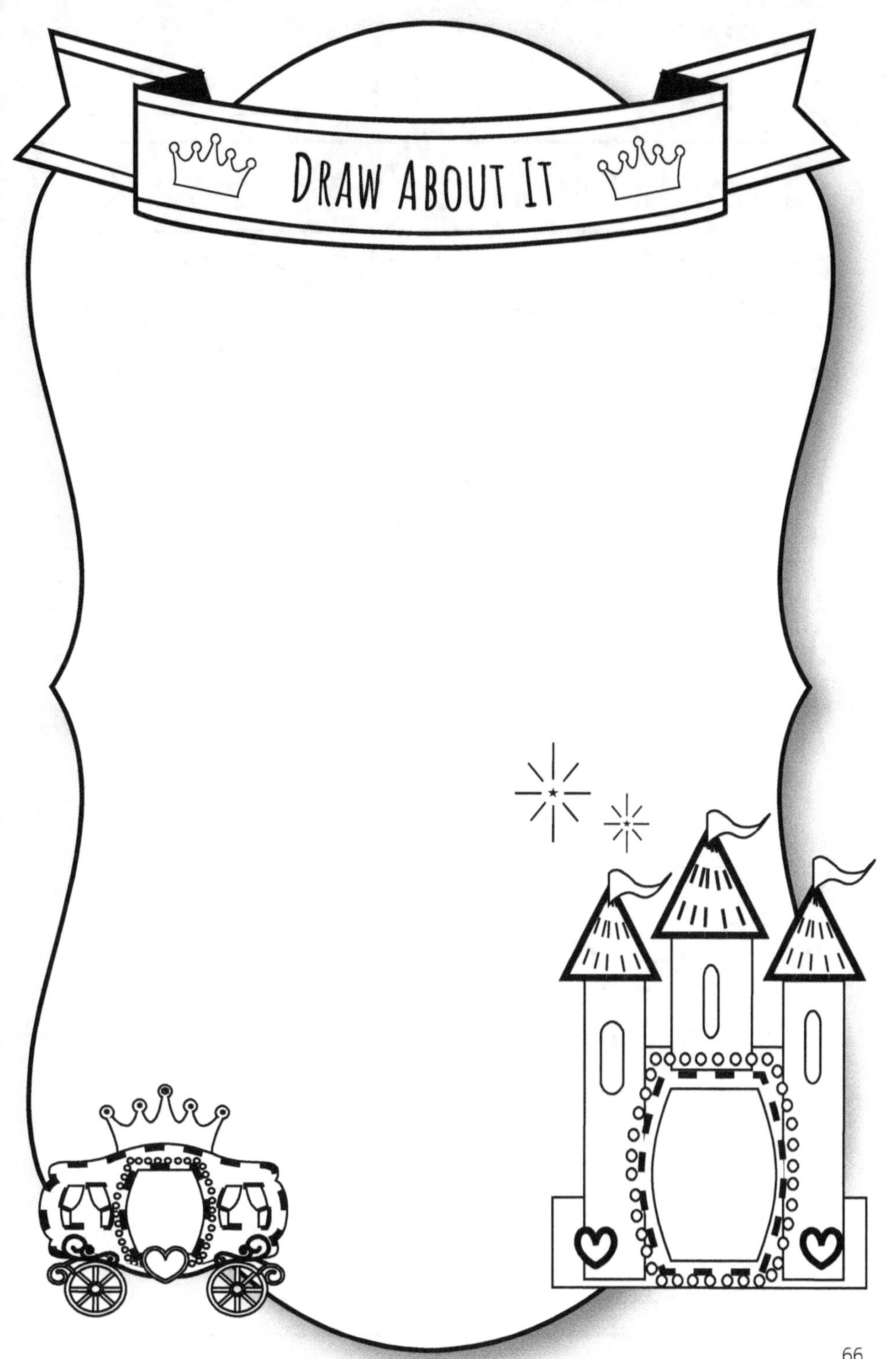

DRAW ABOUT IT

DATE: S M T W TH F S __ / __ / __

OVERALL TODAY WAS: ⭐ ⭐ ⭐ ⭐ ⭐

TODAY'S TRIUMPHS

TODAY'S CHALLENGES

WHAT I LEARNED FROM TODAY:

MY TOP GOAL FOR TOMORROW:

Draw About It

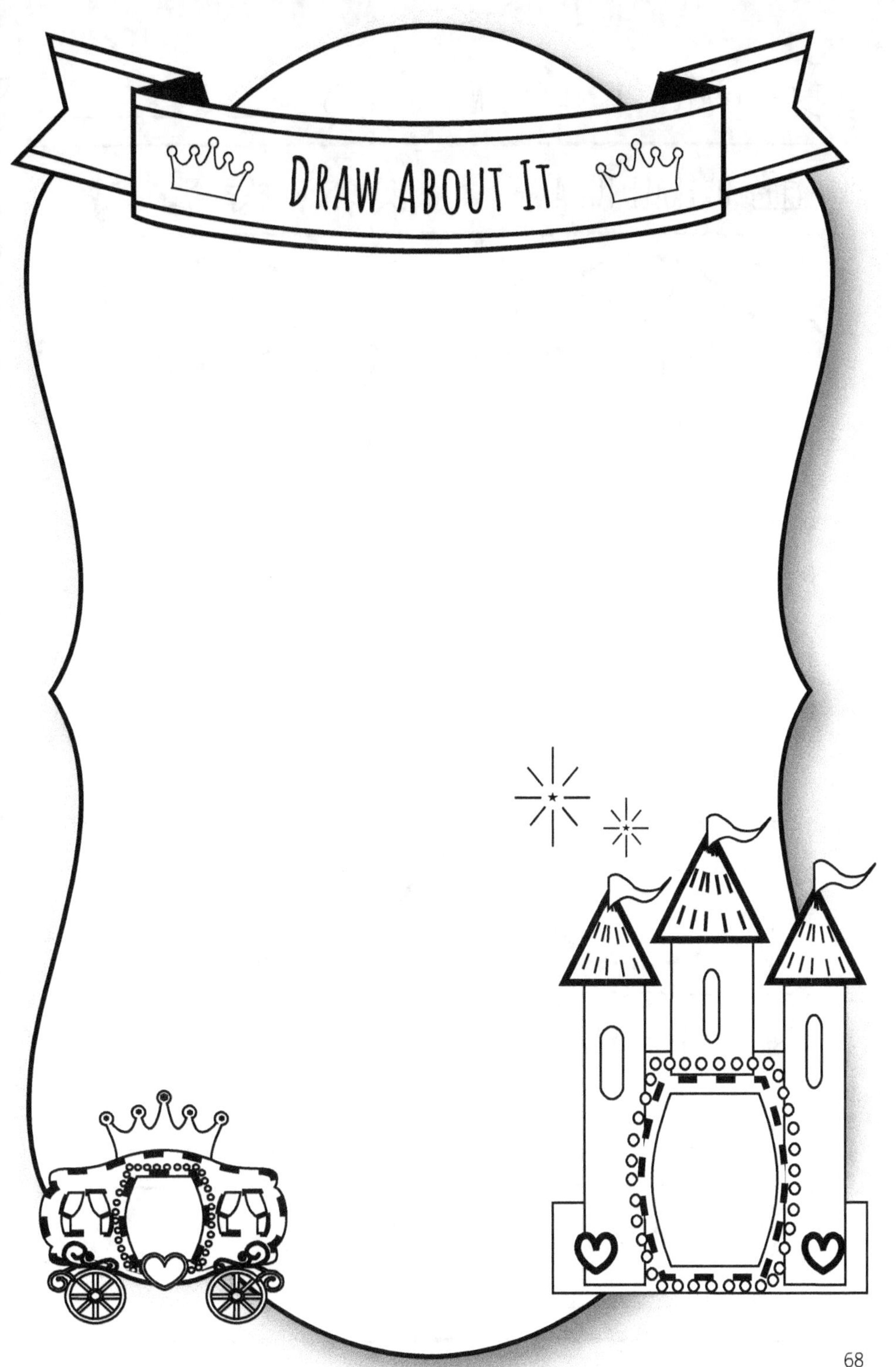

DATE: S M T W TH F S __ / __ / __

OVERALL TODAY WAS: ☆ ☆ ☆ ☆ ☆

👍 TODAY'S TRIUMPHS

👎 TODAY'S CHALLENGES

💡 WHAT I LEARNED FROM TODAY:

🏆 MY TOP GOAL FOR TOMORROW:

Draw About It

DATE: S M T W TH F S __ / __ / __

OVERALL TODAY WAS: ☆ ☆ ☆ ☆ ☆

TODAY'S TRIUMPHS

TODAY'S CHALLENGES

WHAT I LEARNED FROM TODAY:

MY TOP GOAL FOR TOMORROW:

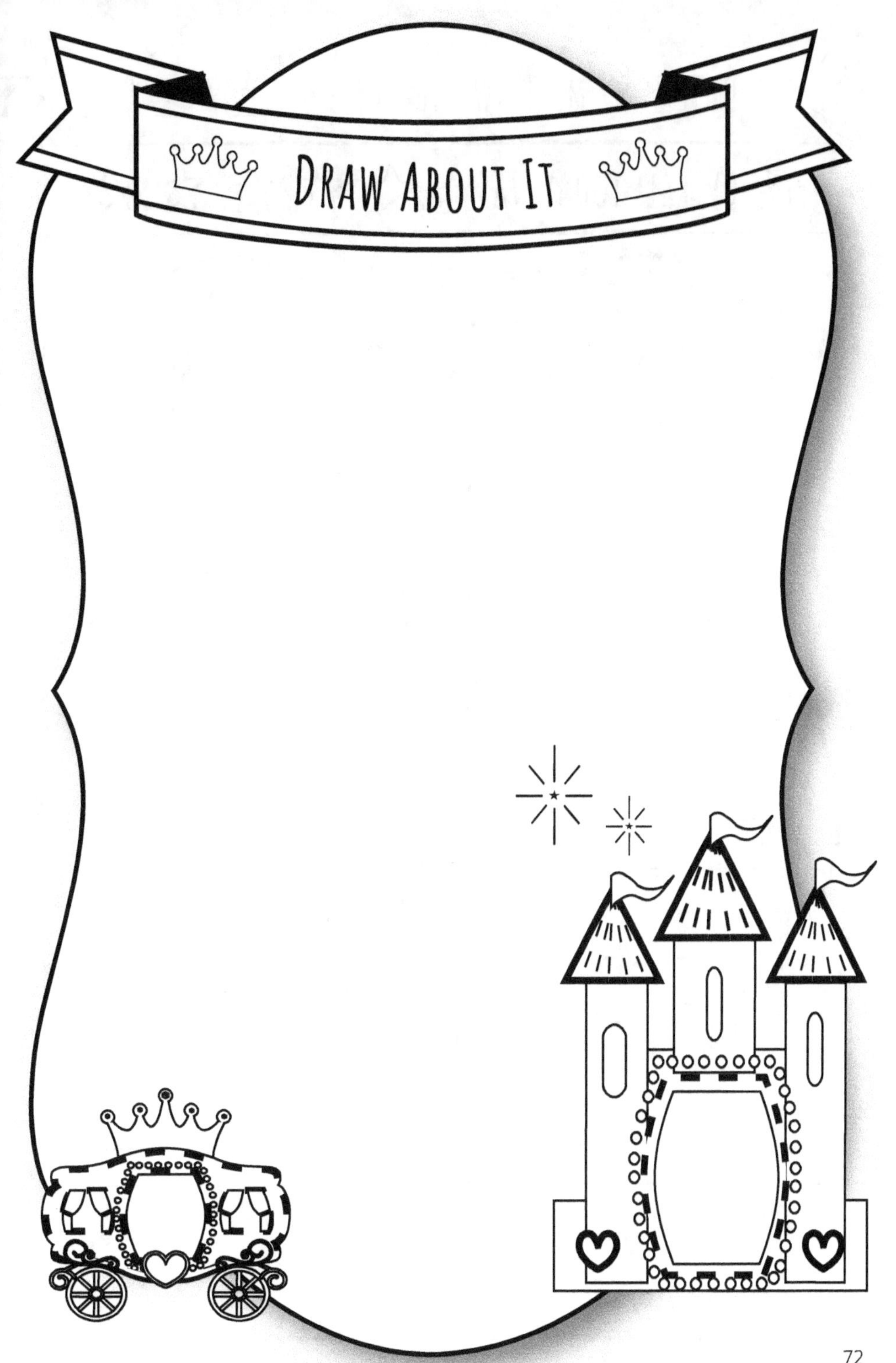

DRAW ABOUT IT

DATE: S M T W TH F S __ / __ / __

OVERALL TODAY WAS: ☆ ☆ ☆ ☆ ☆

👍 TODAY'S TRIUMPHS

👎 TODAY'S CHALLENGES

💡 WHAT I LEARNED FROM TODAY:

🏆 MY TOP GOAL FOR TOMORROW:

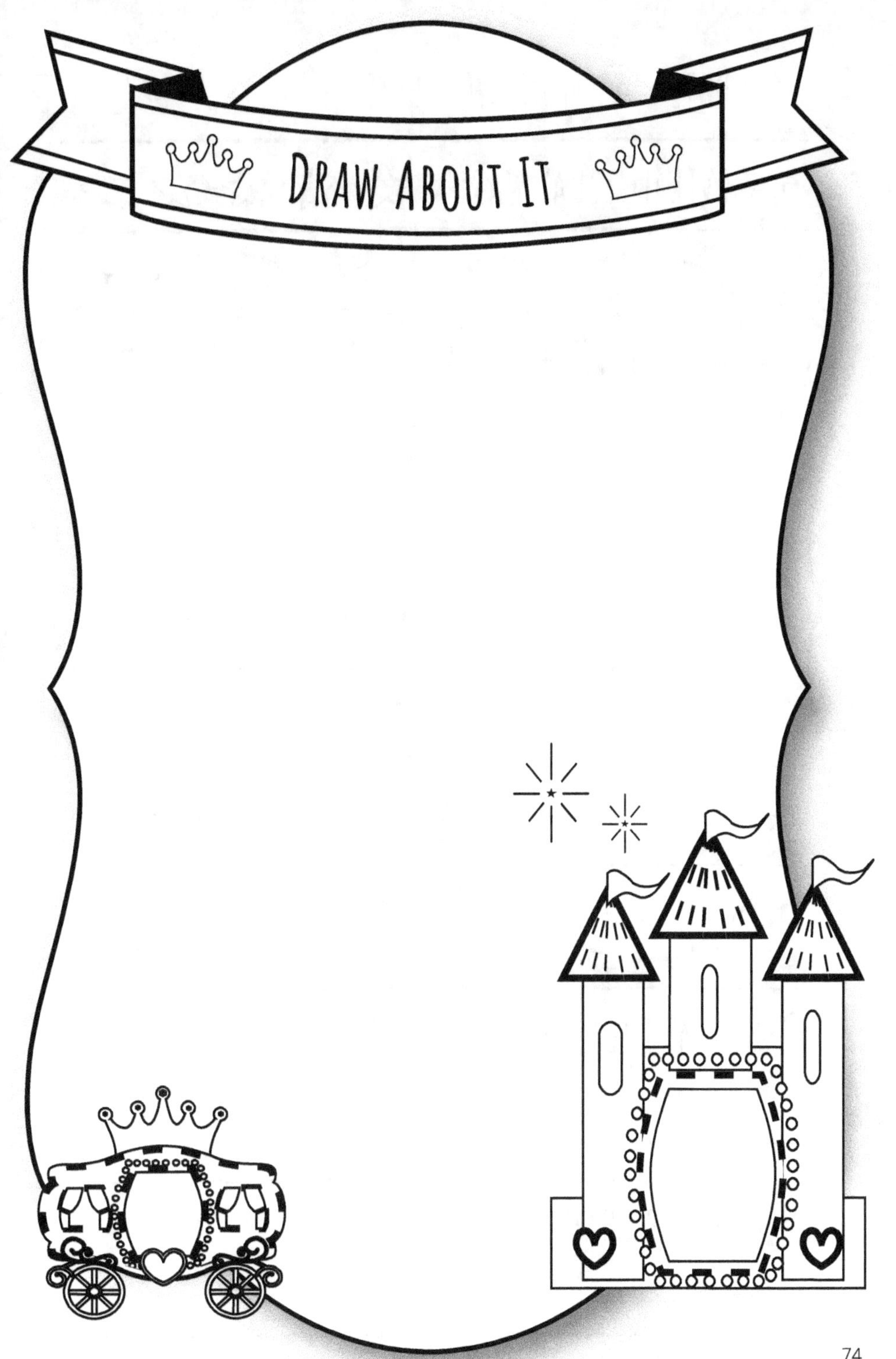

DRAW ABOUT IT

DATE: S M T W TH F S __ / __ / __

🏆 OVERALL TODAY WAS: ☆ ☆ ☆ ☆ ☆

👍 TODAY'S TRIUMPHS

👎 TODAY'S CHALLENGES

💡 WHAT I LEARNED FROM TODAY:

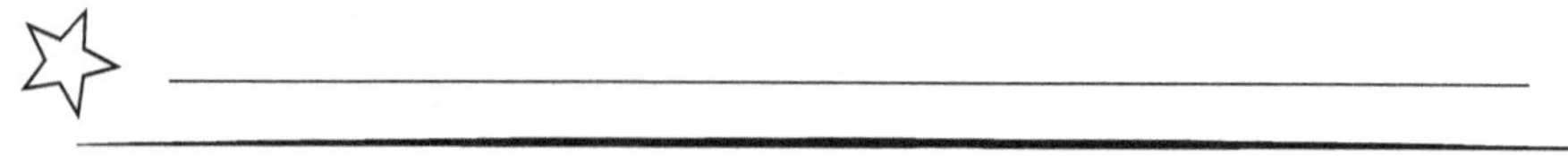

🏆 MY TOP GOAL FOR TOMORROW:

Draw About It

DATE: S M T W TH F S __ / __ / __

OVERALL TODAY WAS: ☆ ☆ ☆ ☆ ☆

TODAY'S TRIUMPHS

TODAY'S CHALLENGES

WHAT I LEARNED FROM TODAY:

MY TOP GOAL FOR TOMORROW:

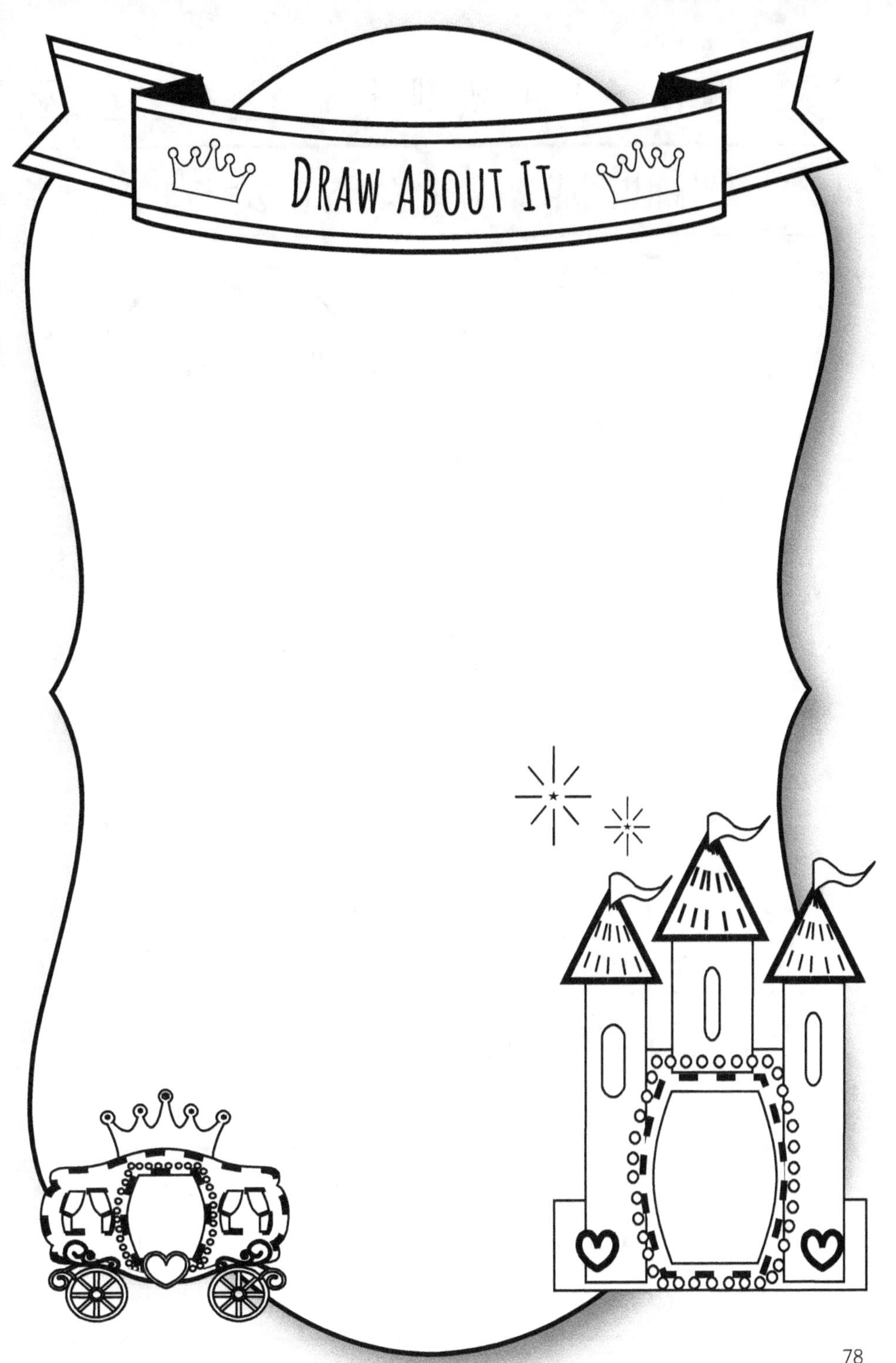DRAW ABOUT IT

DATE: S M T W TH F S   __ / __ / __

TODAY'S TRIUMPHS

TODAY'S CHALLENGES

WHAT I LEARNED FROM TODAY:

MY TOP GOAL FOR TOMORROW:

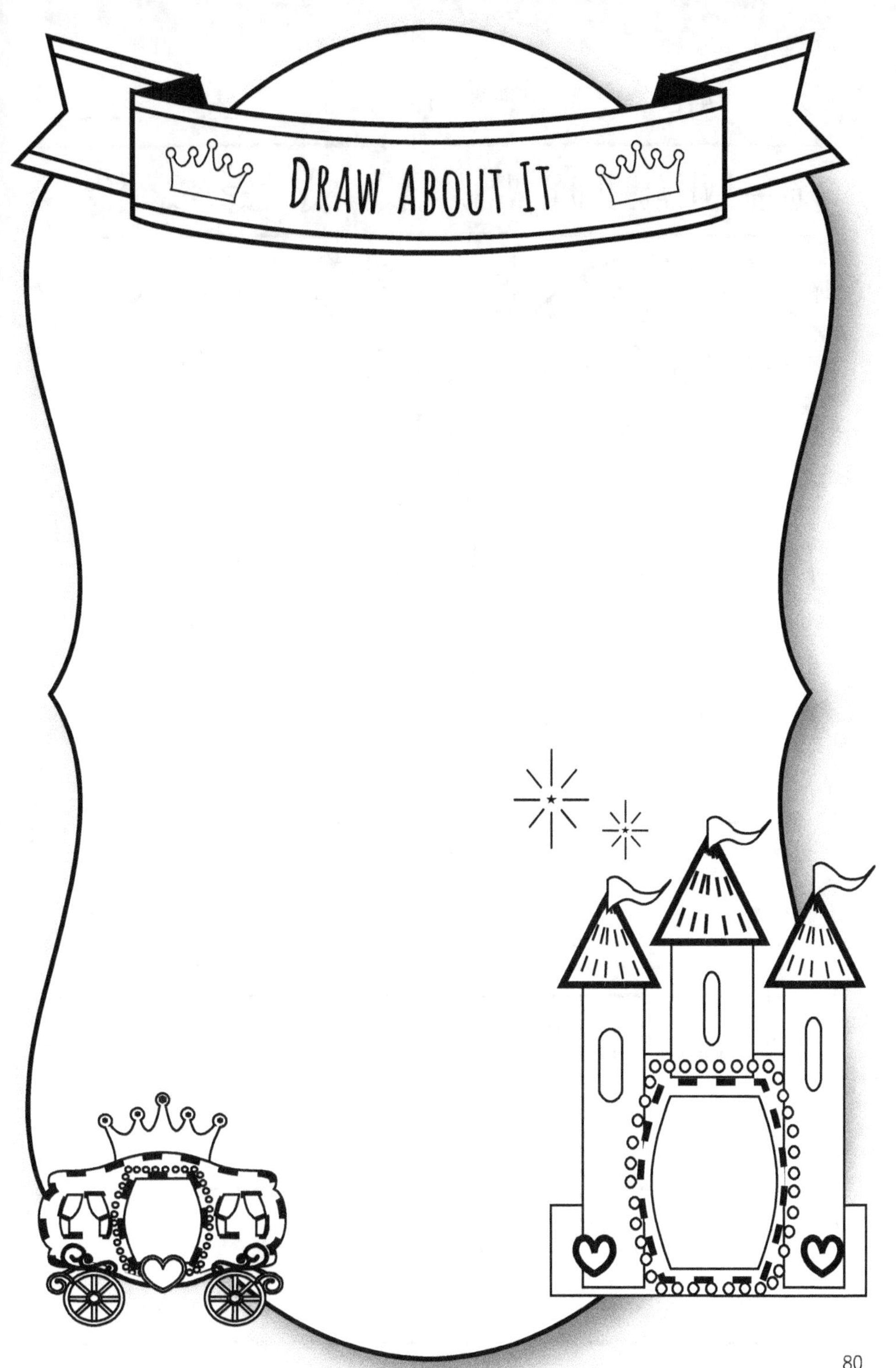

DRAW ABOUT IT

DATE: S M T W TH F S   __ / __ / __

🏆 OVERALL TODAY WAS: ☆ ☆ ☆ ☆ ☆

👍 TODAY'S TRIUMPHS

____
____
____
____
____
____
____
____
____

👎 TODAY'S CHALLENGES

____
____
____
____
____
____
____
____
____

💡 WHAT I LEARNED FROM TODAY:

____
____

🏆 MY TOP GOAL FOR TOMORROW:

____
____

Draw About It

DATE: S M T W TH F S __ / __ / __

OVERALL TODAY WAS: ☆ ☆ ☆ ☆ ☆

👍 TODAY'S TRIUMPHS

👎 TODAY'S CHALLENGES

💡 WHAT I LEARNED FROM TODAY:

🏆 MY TOP GOAL FOR TOMORROW:

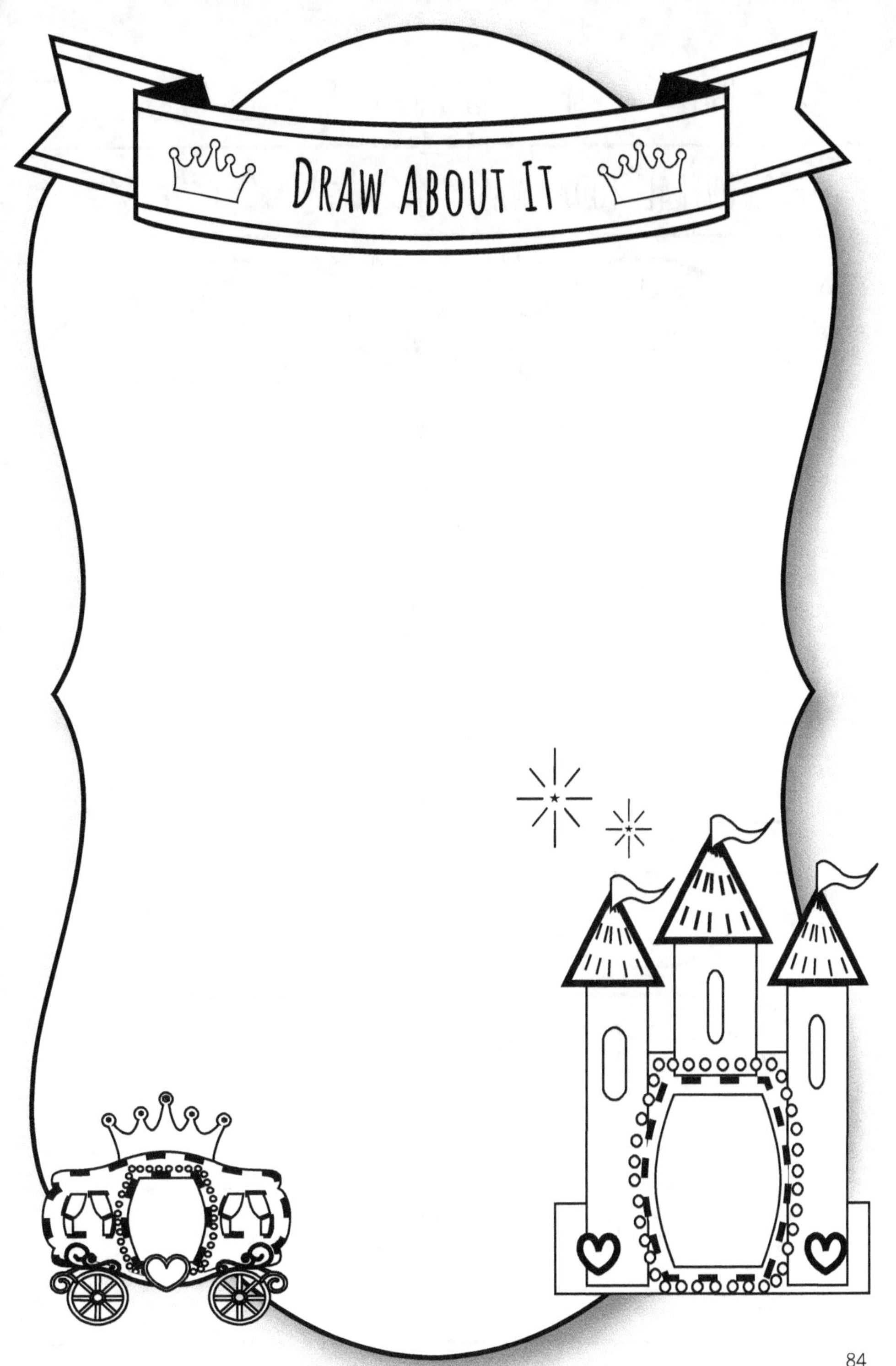

DRAW ABOUT IT

DATE: S M T W TH F S __ / __ / __

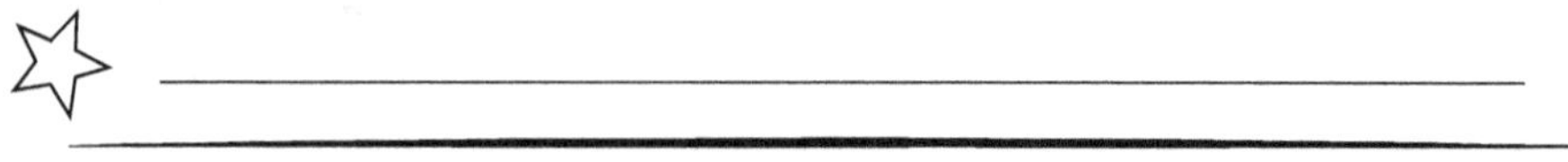

OVERALL TODAY WAS: ☆ ☆ ☆ ☆ ☆

👍 TODAY'S TRIUMPHS

👎 TODAY'S CHALLENGES

💡 WHAT I LEARNED FROM TODAY:

🏆 MY TOP GOAL FOR TOMORROW:

DRAW ABOUT IT

DATE: S M T W TH F S __/__/__

🏆 OVERALL TODAY WAS: ☆ ☆ ☆ ☆ ☆

👍 TODAY'S TRIUMPHS

👎 TODAY'S CHALLENGES

💡 WHAT I LEARNED FROM TODAY:

🏆 MY TOP GOAL FOR TOMORROW:

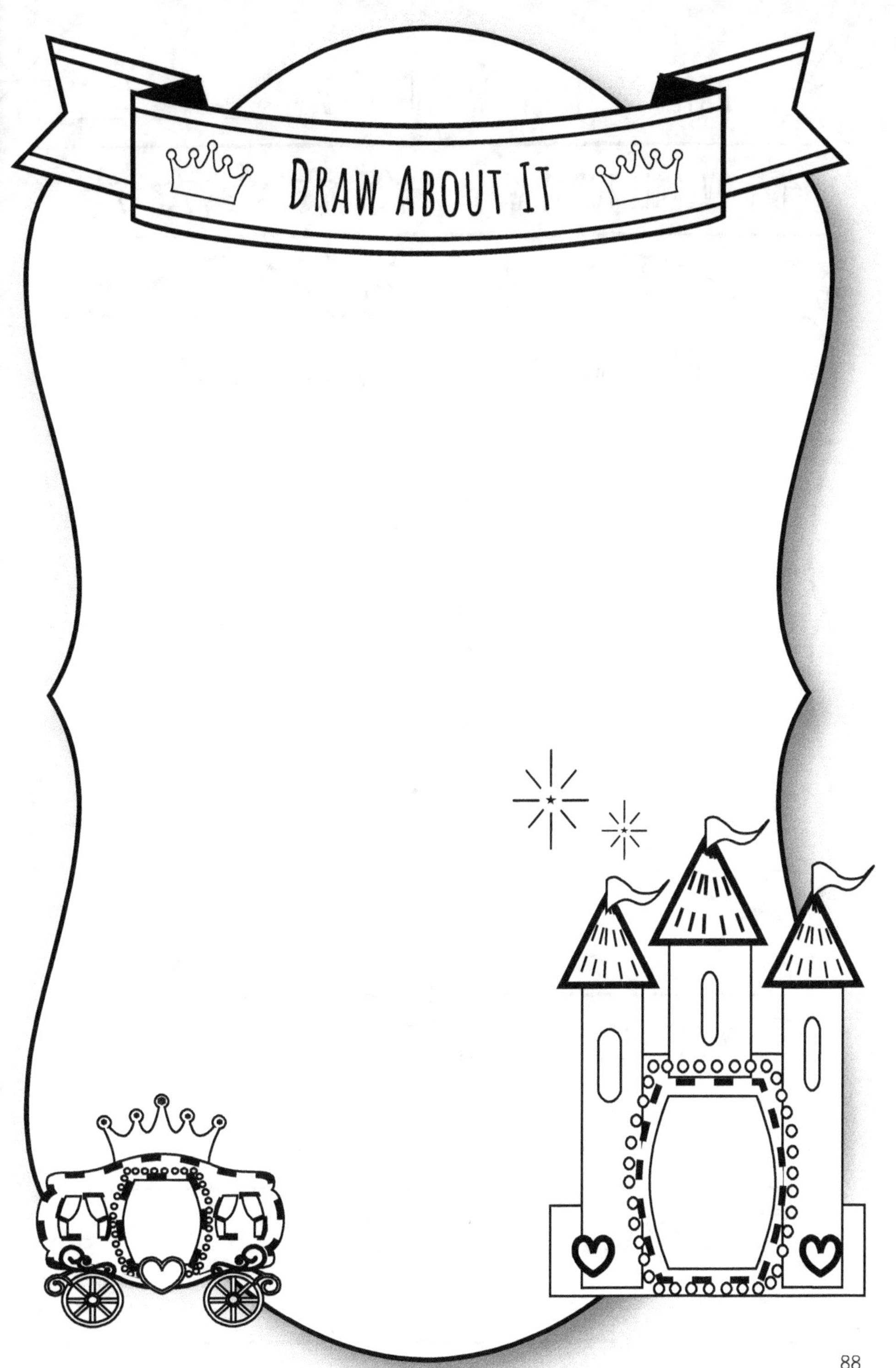

Draw About It

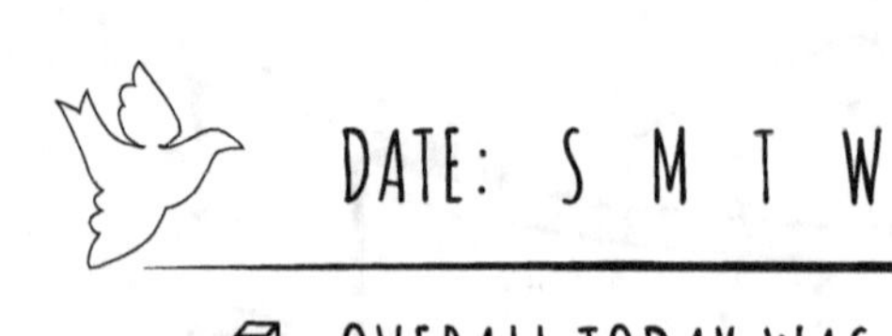 DATE: S M T W TH F S __ / __ / __

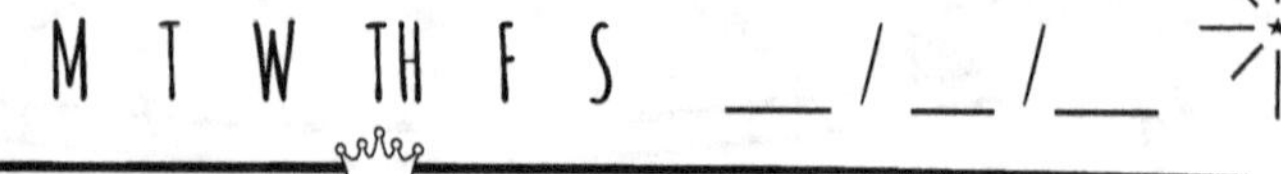

OVERALL TODAY WAS: ⭐ ⭐ ⭐ ⭐ ⭐

👍 TODAY'S TRIUMPHS

👎 TODAY'S CHALLENGES

💡 WHAT I LEARNED FROM TODAY:

 MY TOP GOAL FOR TOMORROW:

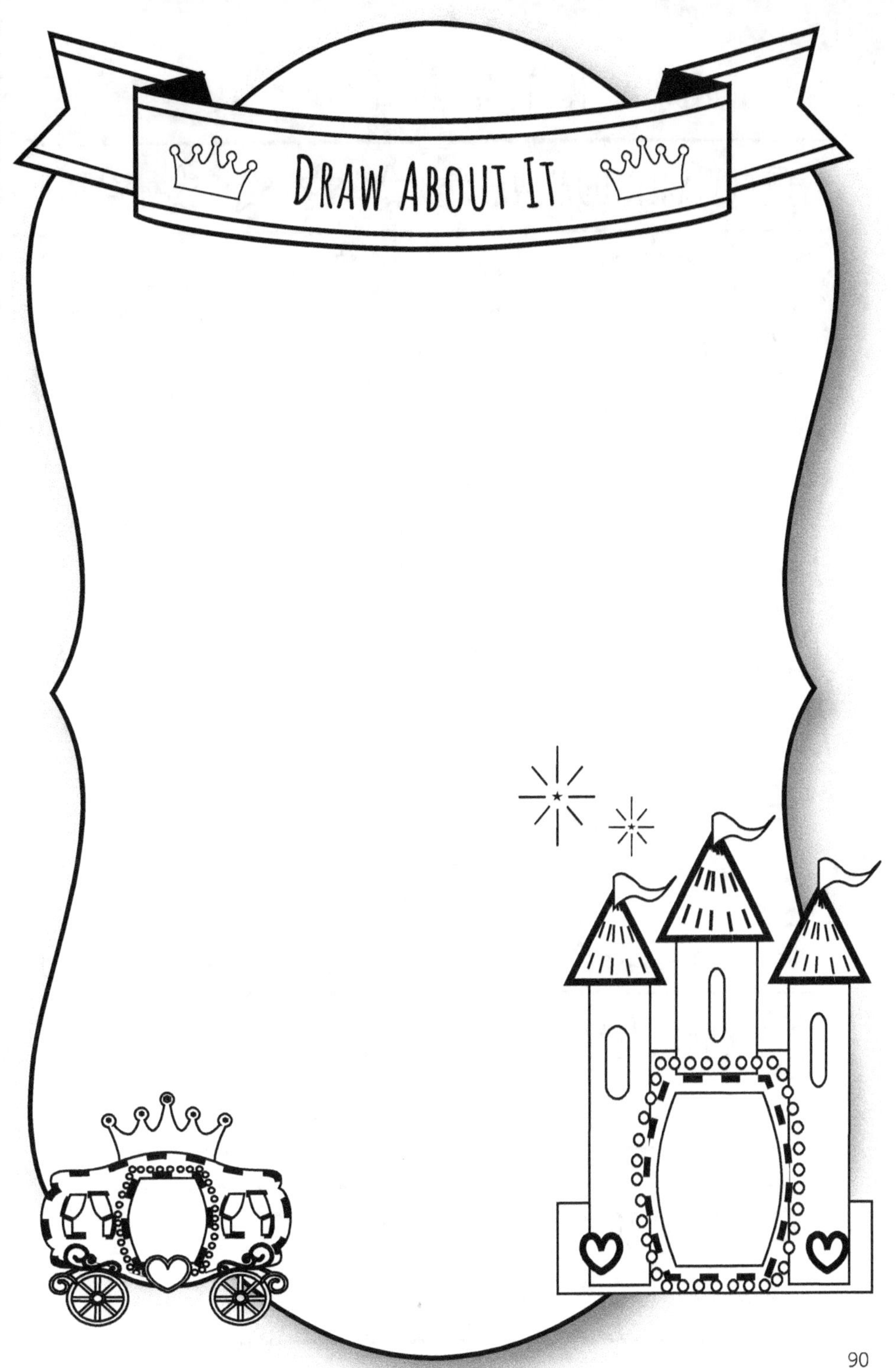
Draw About It

DATE: S M T W TH F S __ / __ / __

 OVERALL TODAY WAS: ☆ ☆ ☆ ☆ ☆

👍 TODAY'S TRIUMPHS

👎 TODAY'S CHALLENGES

💡 WHAT I LEARNED FROM TODAY:

🏆 MY TOP GOAL FOR TOMORROW:

Draw About It

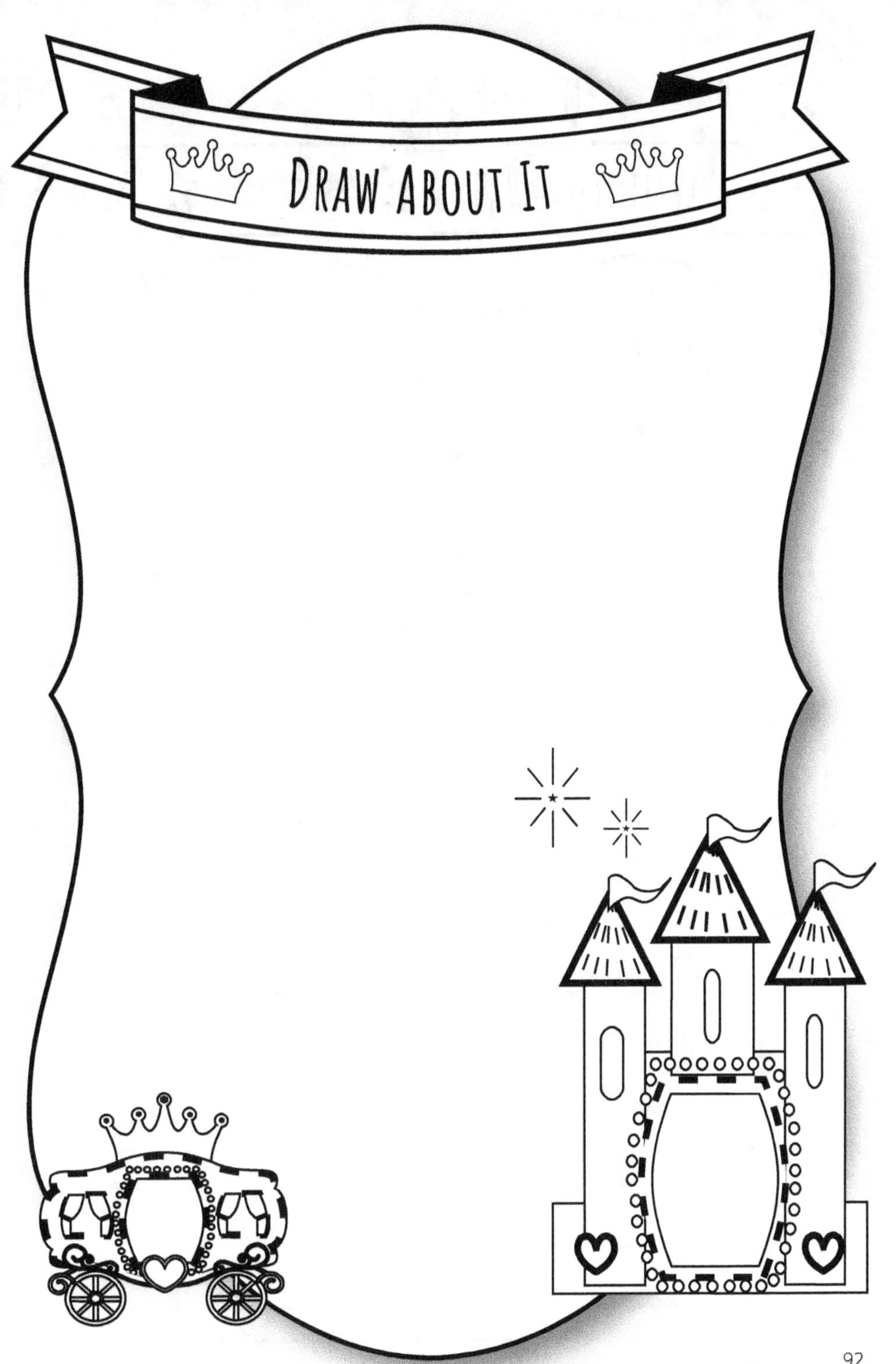

DATE: S M T W TH F S __ / __ / __

OVERALL TODAY WAS: ☆ ☆ ☆ ☆ ☆

👍 TODAY'S TRIUMPHS

👎 TODAY'S CHALLENGES

💡 WHAT I LEARNED FROM TODAY:

🏆 MY TOP GOAL FOR TOMORROW:

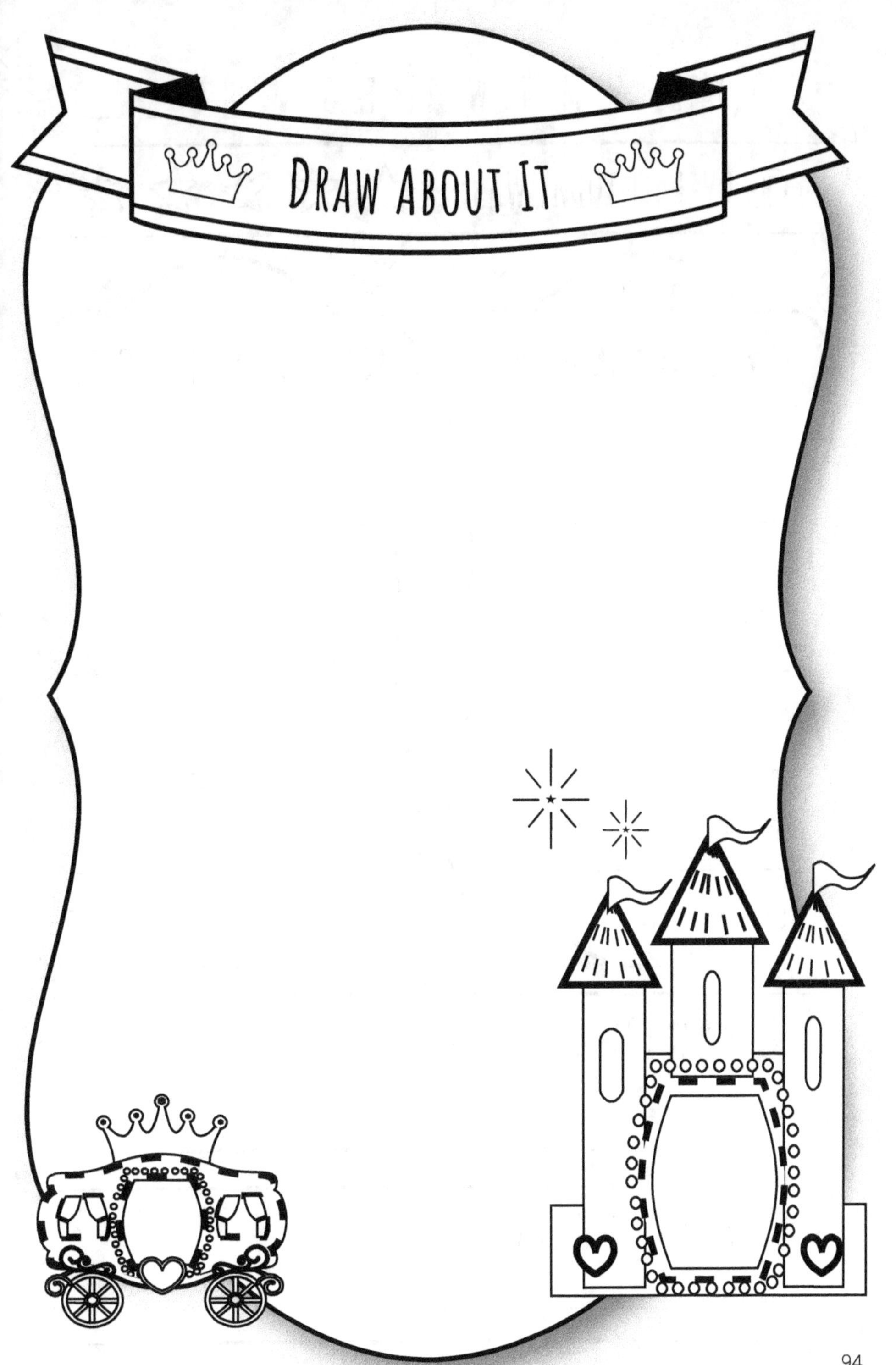

DRAW ABOUT IT

DATE: S M T W TH F S __ / __ / __

🏆 OVERALL TODAY WAS: ★ ★ ★ ★ ★

👍 TODAY'S TRIUMPHS

👎 TODAY'S CHALLENGES

💡 WHAT I LEARNED FROM TODAY:

🏆 MY TOP GOAL FOR TOMORROW:

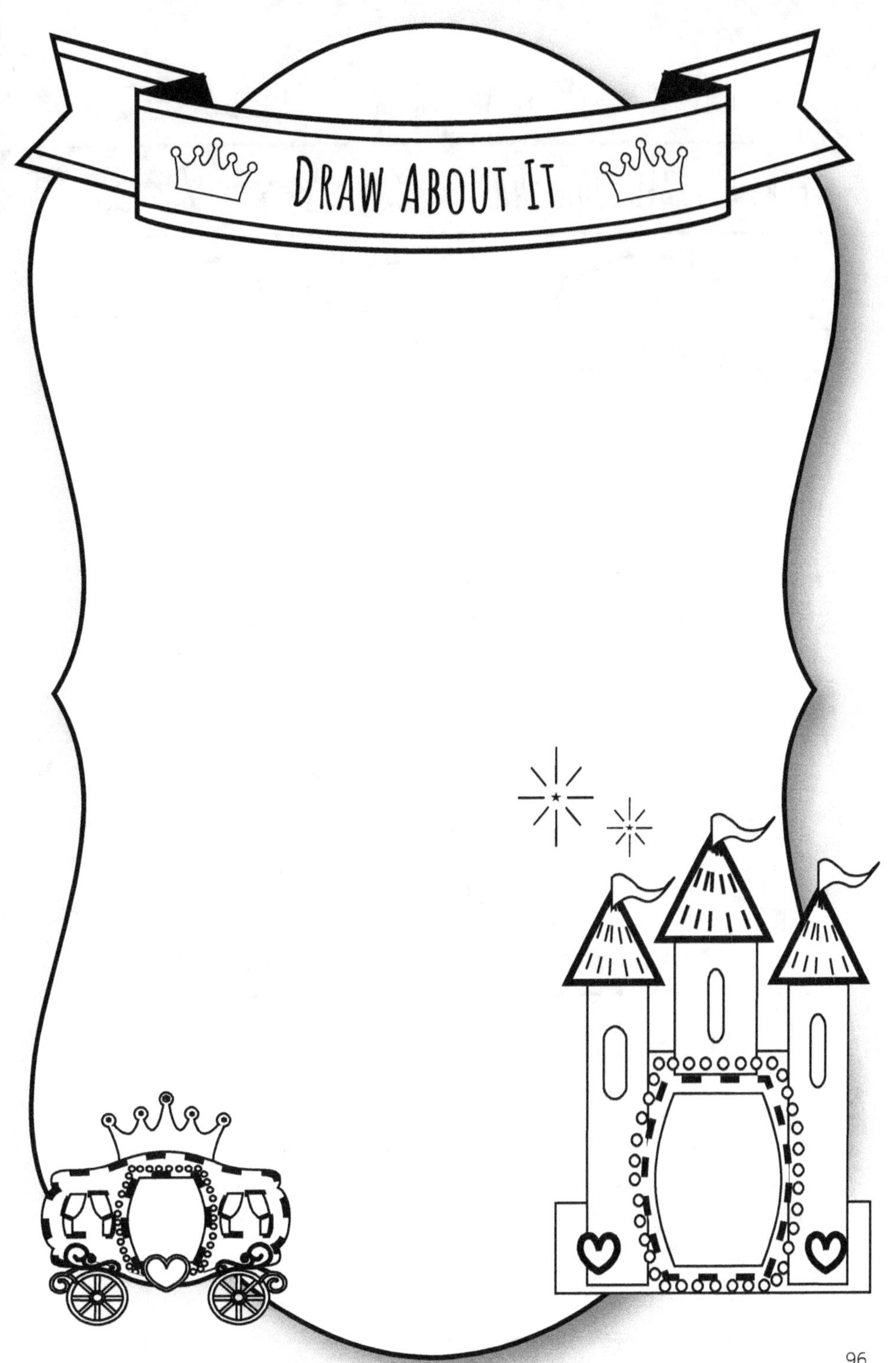

Draw About It

DATE: S M T W TH F S __ / __ / __

🏆 OVERALL TODAY WAS: ☆ ☆ ☆ ☆ ☆

👍 TODAY'S TRIUMPHS

____
____
____
____
____
____
____
____
____
____
____

👎 TODAY'S CHALLENGES

____
____
____
____
____
____
____
____
____
____

💡 WHAT I LEARNED FROM TODAY:

____
____

🏆 MY TOP GOAL FOR TOMORROW:

____
____

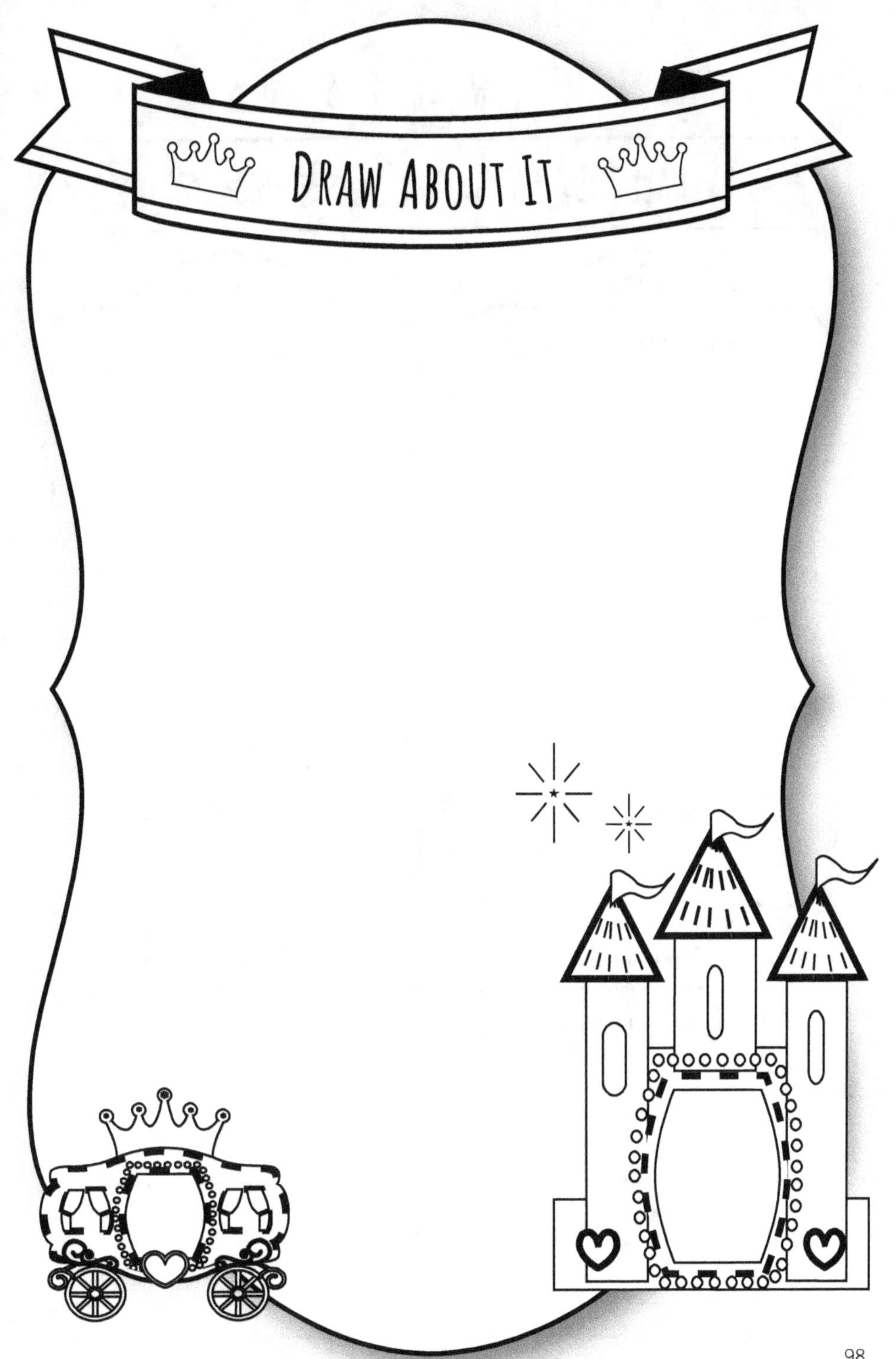

Draw About It

DATE: S M T W TH F S __ / __ / __

🏆 OVERALL TODAY WAS: ☆ ☆ ☆ ☆ ☆

👍 TODAY'S TRIUMPHS

👎 TODAY'S CHALLENGES

💡 WHAT I LEARNED FROM TODAY:

🏆 MY TOP GOAL FOR TOMORROW:

DRAW ABOUT IT

DATE: S M T W TH F S __ / __ / __

OVERALL TODAY WAS: ☆ ☆ ☆ ☆ ☆

TODAY'S TRIUMPHS

TODAY'S CHALLENGES

WHAT I LEARNED FROM TODAY:

MY TOP GOAL FOR TOMORROW:

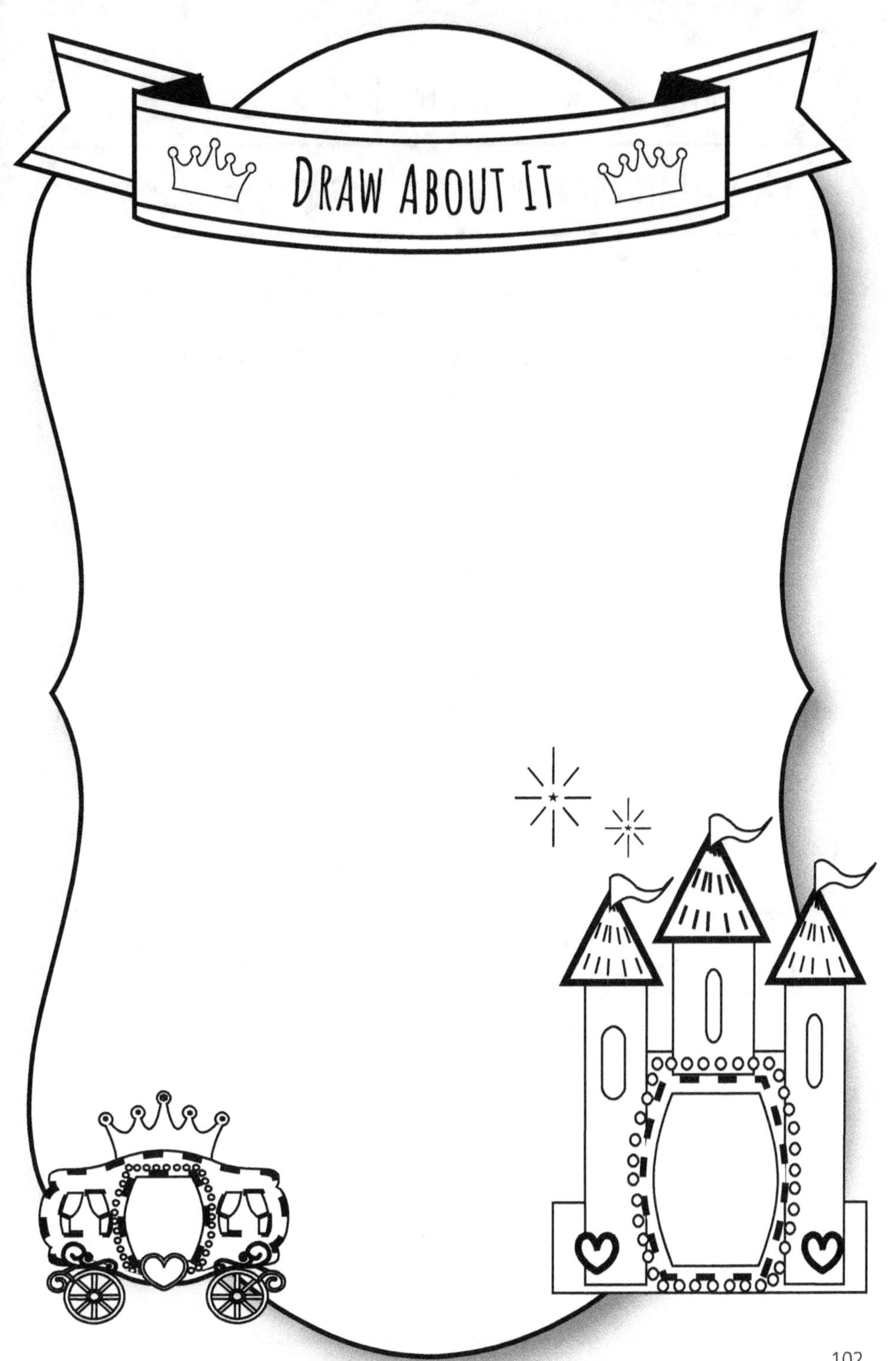
Draw About It

DATE: S M T W TH F S __ / __ / __

OVERALL TODAY WAS: ☆ ☆ ☆ ☆ ☆

TODAY'S TRIUMPHS

TODAY'S CHALLENGES

WHAT I LEARNED FROM TODAY:

MY TOP GOAL FOR TOMORROW:

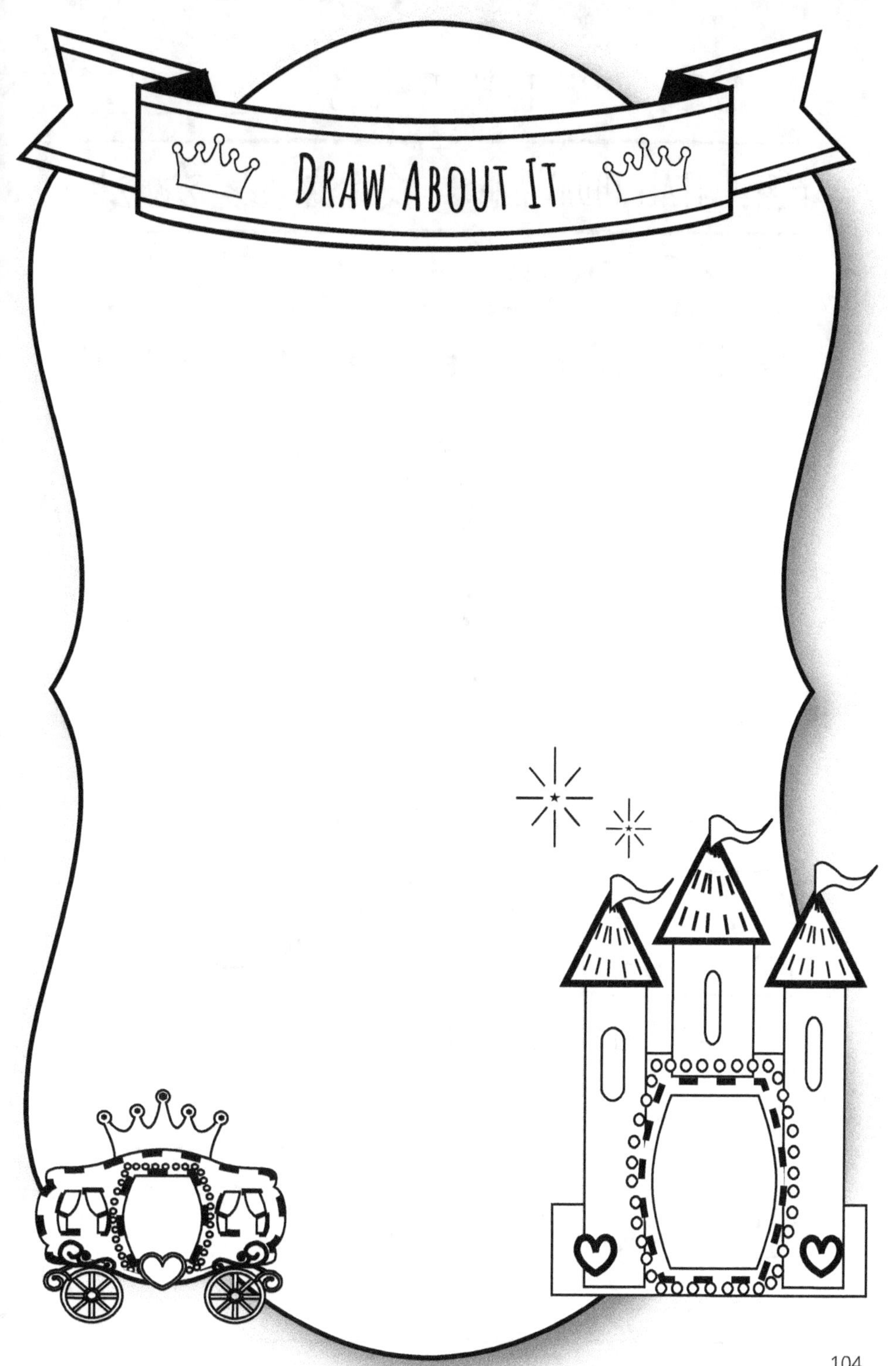

DRAW ABOUT IT

DATE: S M T W TH F S   __ / __ / __

OVERALL TODAY WAS: ☆ ☆ ☆ ☆ ☆

TODAY'S TRIUMPHS

TODAY'S CHALLENGES

WHAT I LEARNED FROM TODAY:

MY TOP GOAL FOR TOMORROW:

Draw About It

DATE: S M T W TH F S __ / __ / __

OVERALL TODAY WAS: ☆ ☆ ☆ ☆ ☆

TODAY'S TRIUMPHS

TODAY'S CHALLENGES

WHAT I LEARNED FROM TODAY:

MY TOP GOAL FOR TOMORROW:

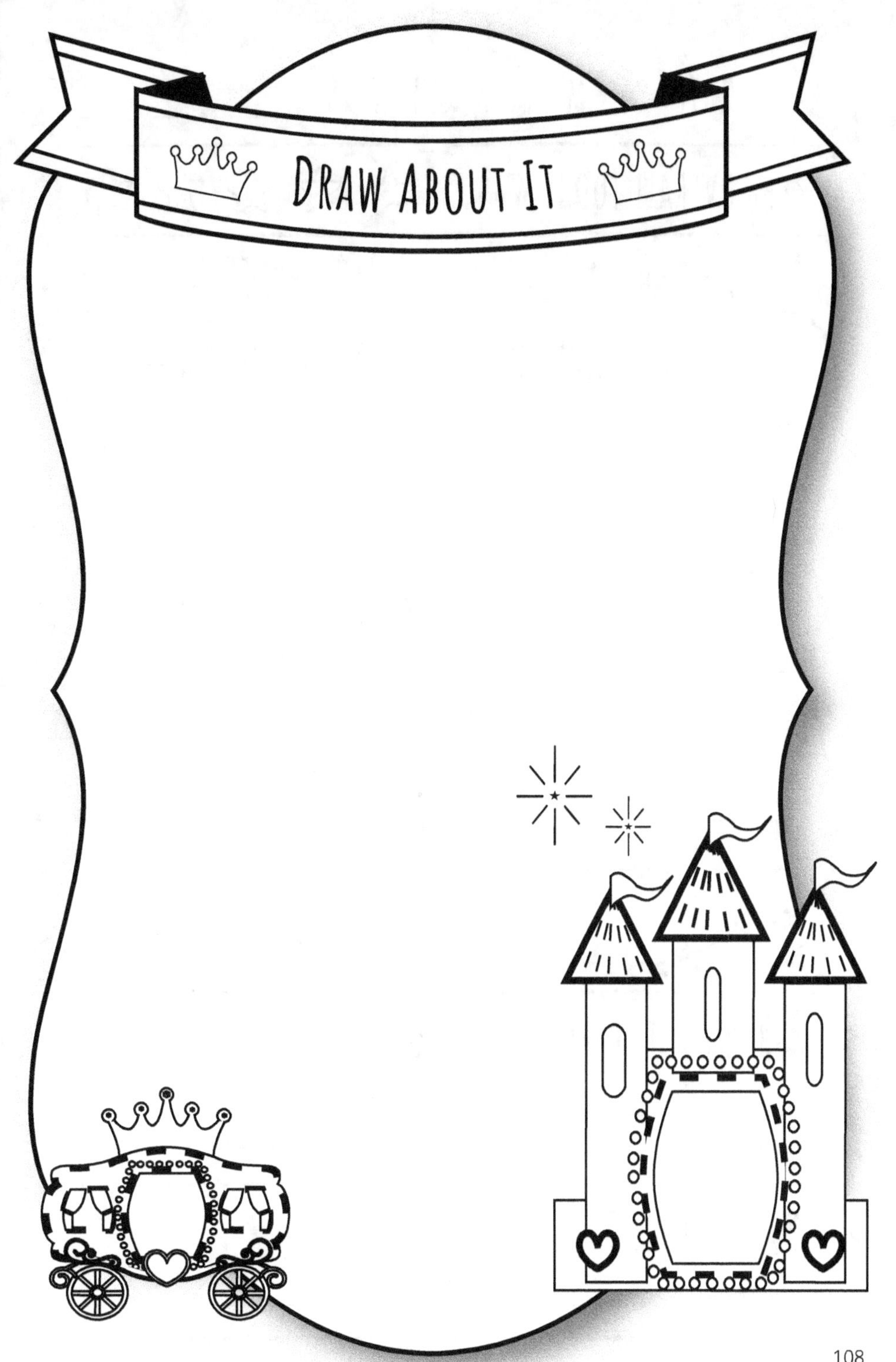
DRAW ABOUT IT

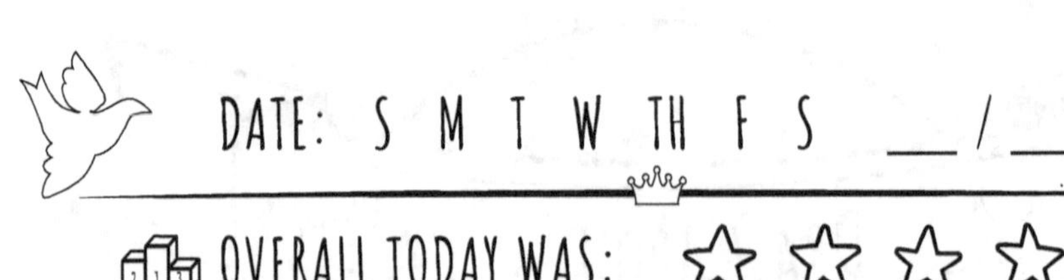

DATE: S M T W TH F S __ / __ / __

OVERALL TODAY WAS: ☆ ☆ ☆ ☆ ☆

👍 TODAY'S TRIUMPHS

👎 TODAY'S CHALLENGES

💡 WHAT I LEARNED FROM TODAY:

🏆 MY TOP GOAL FOR TOMORROW:

DRAW ABOUT IT

DATE: S M T W TH F S __/__/__

OVERALL TODAY WAS: ☆ ☆ ☆ ☆ ☆

TODAY'S TRIUMPHS

TODAY'S CHALLENGES

WHAT I LEARNED FROM TODAY:

MY TOP GOAL FOR TOMORROW:

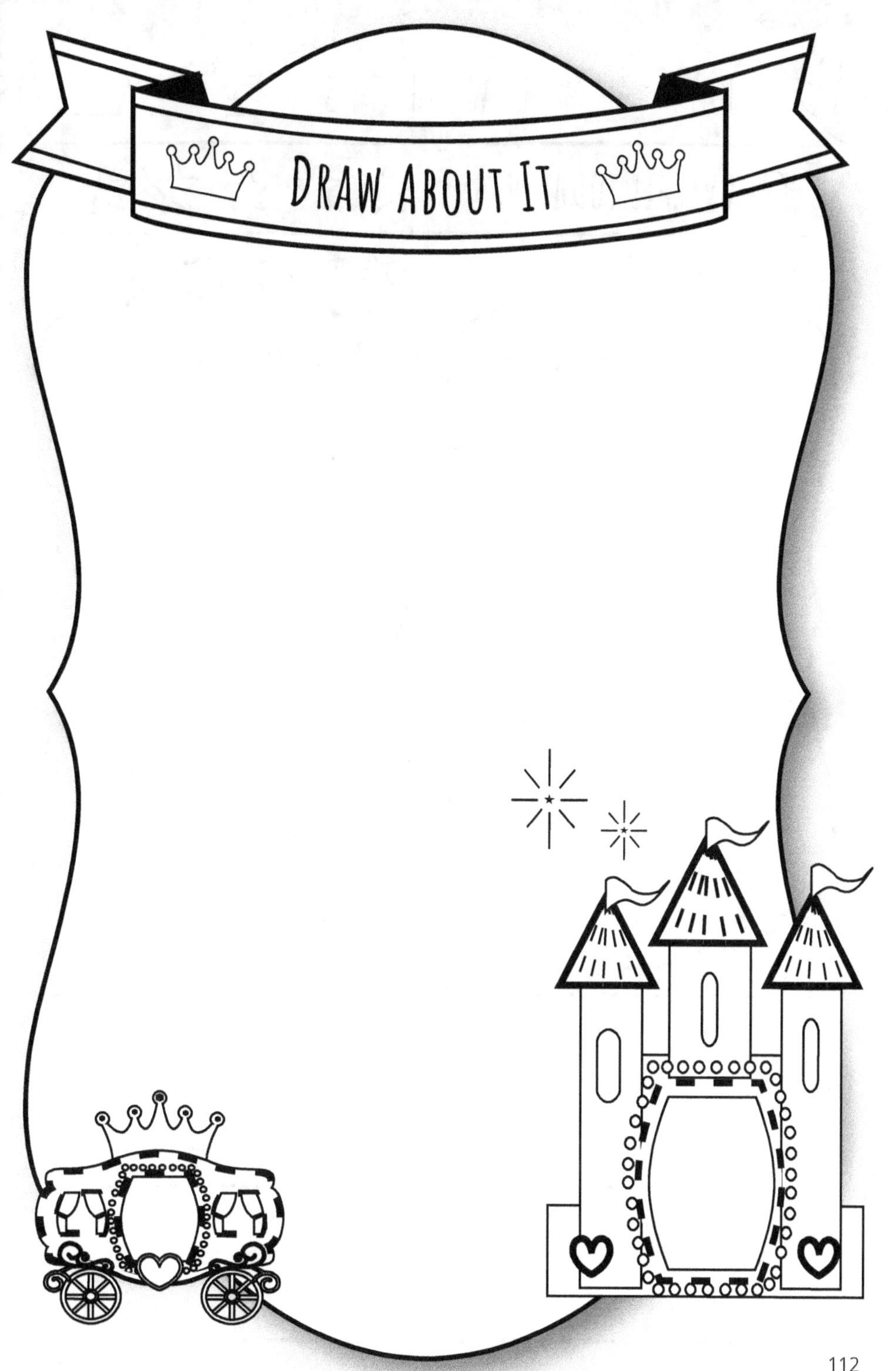

DRAW ABOUT IT

DATE: S M T W TH F S __ / __ / __

OVERALL TODAY WAS: ☆ ☆ ☆ ☆ ☆

👍 TODAY'S TRIUMPHS

👎 TODAY'S CHALLENGES

💡 WHAT I LEARNED FROM TODAY:

🏆 MY TOP GOAL FOR TOMORROW:

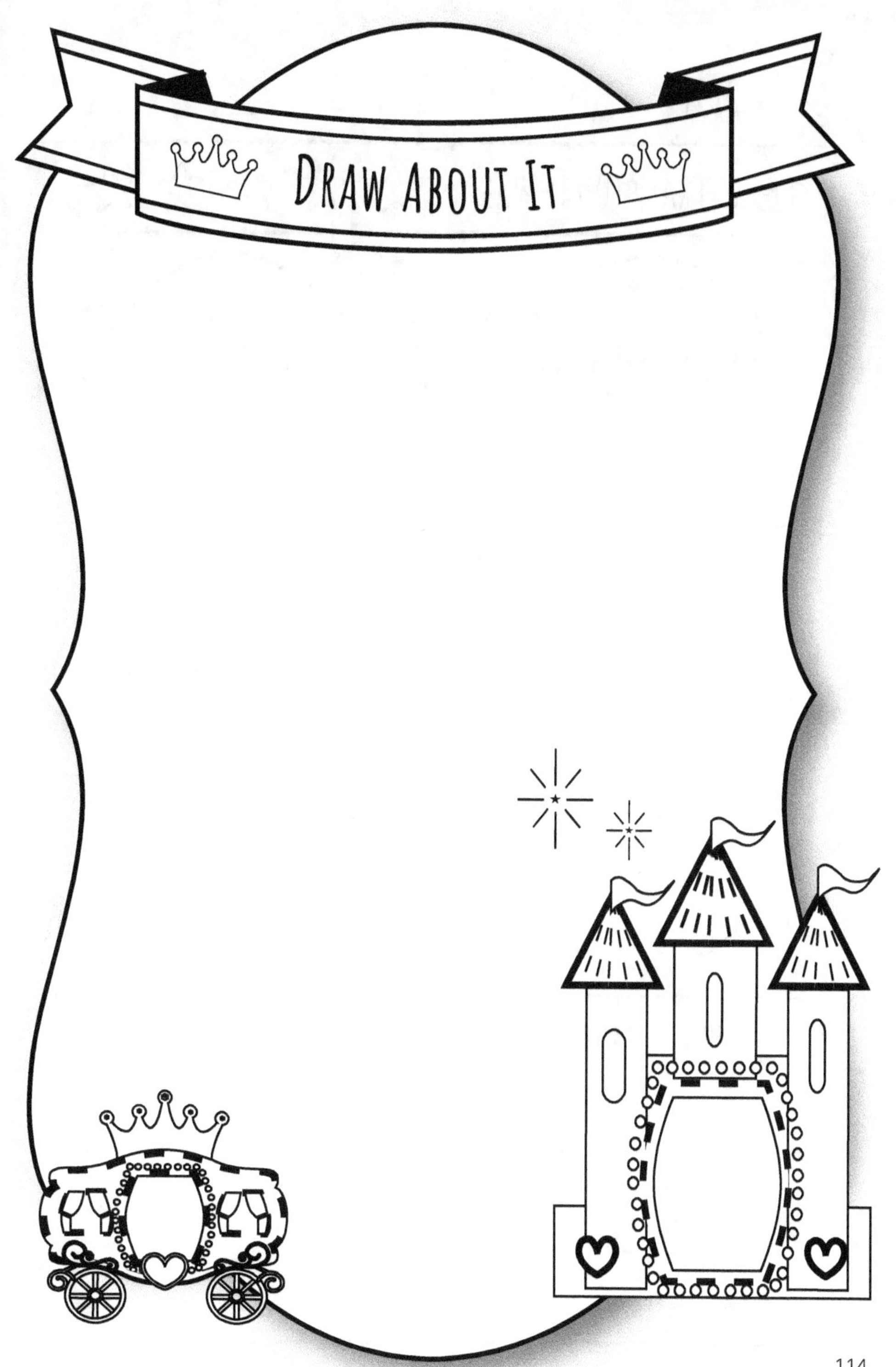
Draw About It

DATE: S M T W TH F S __ / __ / __

OVERALL TODAY WAS:

👍 TODAY'S TRIUMPHS

👎 TODAY'S CHALLENGES

💡 WHAT I LEARNED FROM TODAY:

🏆 MY TOP GOAL FOR TOMORROW:

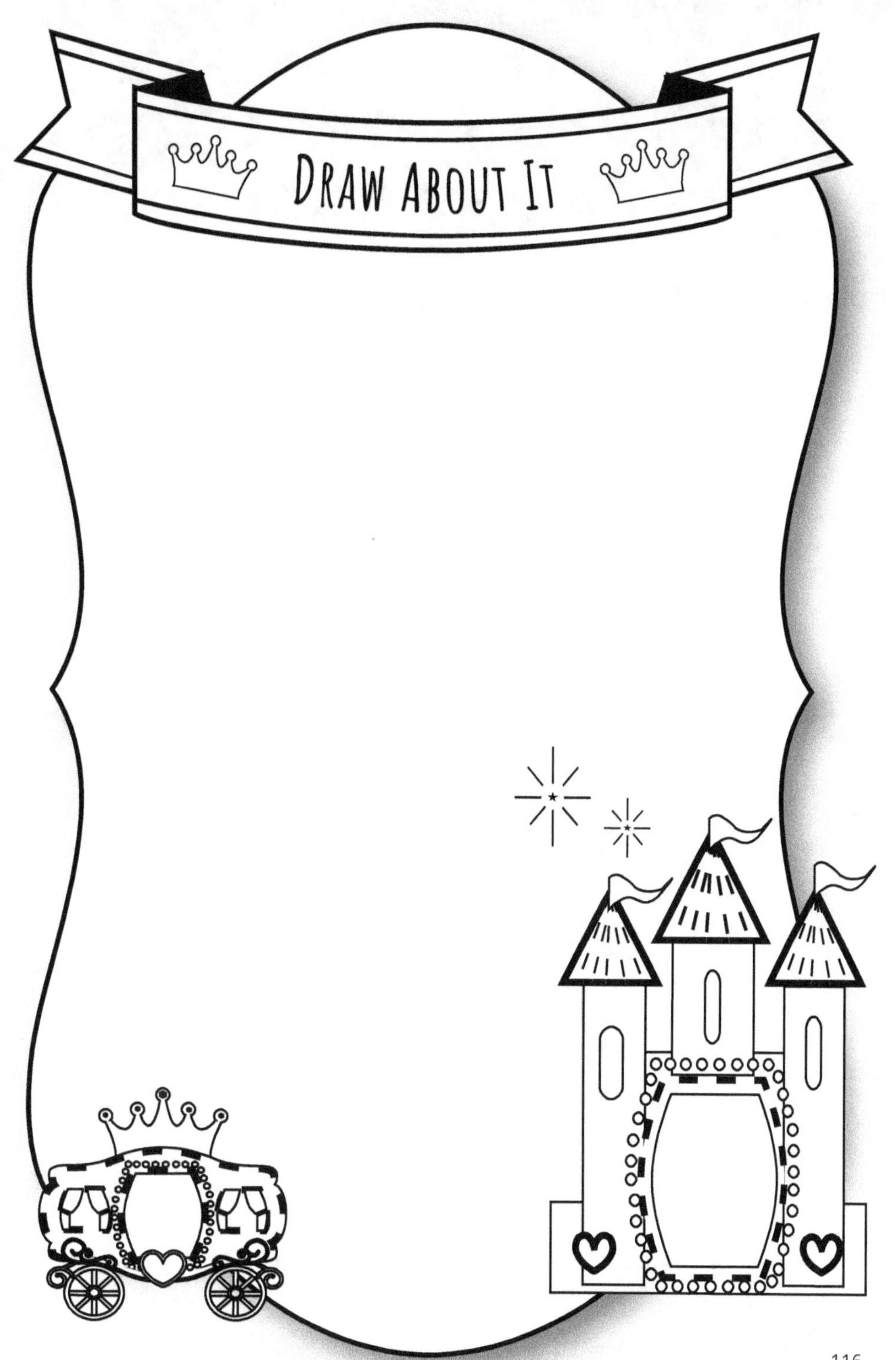

DRAW ABOUT IT

9 781774 761854